How Mystics

Can Unify

Science

and

Religion

From the Heart of Jesus, vol 7

How Mystics Can Unify Science

and

Religion

KIM MICHAELS

Copyright © 2014 Kim Michaels. All rights reserved. No part of this book may be used, reproduced, translated, electronically stored or transmitted by any means except by written permission from the publisher. A reviewer may quote brief passages in a review.

MORE TO LIFE PUBLISHING

www.morepublish.com

For foreign and translation rights,

contact info@ morepublish.com

ISBN: 978-9949-518-47-0

Series ISBN: 978-9949-518-21-0

The information and insights in this book should not be considered as a form of therapy, advice, direction, diagnosis, and/or treatment of any kind. This information is not a substitute for medical, psychological, or other professional advice, counseling and care. All matters pertaining to your individual health should be supervised by a physician or appropriate health-care practitioner. No guarantee is made by the author or the publisher that the practices described in this book will yield successful results for anyone at any time. They are presented for informational purposes only, as the practice and proof rests with the individual.

For more information:

www.askrealjesus.com

www.transcendencetoolbox.com

CONTENTS

Introduction 7

1 | Who Would Start a Religious War? 11

2 | More than One True Religion? 27

3 | The True Purpose of Religion 39

4 | The True Purpose of Religious Teachings 55

5 | Why so Many Different Religions? 67

6 | Overcoming the Fear of Change 83

7 | Who Can Stop Religious Conflict? 113

8 | A Nonviolent Approach to Mystical Visions 137

9 | A Mystical Approach to New Ideas 165

10 | A Nonviolent Approach to Religion 177

11 | Unity Without Sameness 203

12 | Religion and Science 215

13 | Religious Tolerance 245

14 | Creating False Gods 257

INTRODUCTION

One of the defining questions of my childhood was how the members of the Christian religion could commit atrocities like the Crusades, the Inquisition and the witch hunts. I did not receive a Christian or religious upbringing, but I knew Jesus' true teachings were completely non-violent. How can one then explain that those who claim to follow Jesus have so often turned to violence?

This question and several others sent me on a quest for answers, and it has taken me far beyond traditional sources to what I prefer to call mysticism or the mystical path. I discovered that throughout the ages many men and women have found this path, which runs like a generally unseen thread behind all of the formal religions. The mystical path has several stages, and here are some of them:

- You realize there is more to know about the spiritual side of life than what you have been told by mainstream religions.

- You open your mind to studying material from a variety of sources, letting your intuition guide you.

- You realize that beyond all mainstream religions is a universal mystical path and people have been following it for thousands of years. This path is an inner path of raising your consciousness.

- You realize that mainstream religions demand that you uncritically believe in their doctrines, yet you have a God-given ability to receive insights and understanding from within yourself. These insights come from a higher part of your being and from a group of universal teachers in the spiritual realm.

- You engage in a determined effort to increase your inner, intuitive, mystical connection to something beyond your human mind.

- As you attain mystical experiences, you realize that the real goal of the mystical path is to attain inner union with your own higher being and with one or several spiritual beings.

- As you begin to attain this inner union, you realize you are not actually on earth in order to just get out of here again. You are here to fulfill a specific mission. This mission may involve you helping to bring society forward in various ways, including bringing forth new spiritual teachings from a higher source.

Personally, I have been following the mystical path for a long time, seeking mystical union with my higher self and various spiritual teachers. In 2001 I realized that my primary spiritual teacher is Jesus as he is today, namely an ascended being, an ascended master, who is actively working with humankind.

Introduction

I then started seeking mystical union with Jesus as a natural stage on my personal path.

As I increased my inner union with Jesus, I realized he wanted me to bring forth a website that could correct the many misconceptions about him and his teachings promoted by mainstream Christianity. He wanted there to be a source where people could connect to him as an ascended being and realize he is willing to help today's spiritual seekers. He also wanted to give people a correct view of his mission so they could heal the wounds they have received from Christian churches. Finally, he wanted people to realize that he has much more to teach us today than what he could give 2,000 years ago.

I have since 2002 brought forth a very large body of teachings through a process of mystical revelation. For more information on how this happens, see the first book in this series, *The Mystical Teachings of Jesus* or the website *www.askrealjesus.com*.

1 | WHO WOULD START A RELIGIOUS WAR?

Kim: Jesus, we have a long list of major religious wars or atrocities involving Christians, such as the Crusades, the massacre of the Cathars, the Inquisition and several wars between Catholics and Protestants, one of them lasting a hundred years. We also have a lot of ongoing conflicts that have led to the killing of many people in the name of Christ. If you listen to those who don't like Christianity, as many as 17 million people have been killed by Christians, and even Christians will admit that it is a substantial number. How do you feel about people being killed in your name?

Jesus: Are you implying that I should feel worse about people being killed in the name of Christianity than I should feel about people being killed for other reasons?

I assume that since you told us to turn the other cheek, you would not like Christians killing people in your name. I assume you might feel responsible for having started a religion that has turned out to be one of the most violent religions in recorded history.

That was a lot of assumptions. You assume I founded the religion of Christianity. You assume I started a fear-based religion that found it necessary to use violence in a desperate attempt to kill the fear. You assume I feel responsible for the actions of human beings and that I feel especially responsible for the actions of those who use my name yet don't internalize my teachings. You assume that people have been killed in my name and have been killed by true Christians. Your assumptions are understandable from a human viewpoint, but I hope I can help you see that they are not logical.

But these are assumptions shared by an awful lot of people including many Christians.

My intention here is to help you reach a higher understanding of the cause of religious conflict. If you are willing to open your mind to this higher understanding, you will see why your assumptions are not logical. I realize they seem logical with your present level of understanding, but this raises an essential question.

If you acknowledge that you do not understand the cause of religious conflict, then you should be willing to see that there is only one way for you to get this understanding. Right now you have a certain amount of knowledge and understanding of the world. We might say that your mind forms a box and there are certain contents in the box. Given the size and contents of your mental box, you do not understand the cause of religious conflict. If you are to attain this understanding, you must do something to change the equation. Most people would say that they have to get some knowledge they don't have, meaning they have to put more content into the mental box. While this is not invalid, there is another aspect, namely that you can expand the box. You can raise your mind to a distinctly higher level of consciousness where you can see what you simply cannot see right now. If you are walking in a dense jungle, you cannot see very far for the trees. If you could climb a tower and look above the trees, you would more easily find your way.

As an ascended spiritual teacher I constantly run into the same problem today that I ran into when I walked the earth in a physical body. Why do you think I so often talked about those who have ears to hear? The question is simple: Are you talking to me because you want me to confirm your present opinions, or are you open to the possibility that I could give you a higher understanding that might cause you to revise those opinions?

If you only want to have your present opinions confirmed – as most people do – then I simply cannot help you. I am a spiritual teacher, and I have an uncompromising allegiance to reality—which is a diplomatic way of saying that I will not compromise reality in order to conform to human opinions. Do you want confirmation or do you want understanding?

Yes, please help me understand the cause of religious conflict.

I would like to begin by asking you to consider the following statement:

> Verily I say unto you, Inasmuch as ye have done it unto one of the least of these my brethren, ye have done it unto me. (Matthew 25:40)

This statement was meant to illustrate how I feel when one human being hurts another. If you hurt any other human being, I will feel their pain and suffering. What you do to another human being, you are truly doing to me. What do you think this means?

I don't know, I can't even imagine how you could possibly feel the pain and suffering of every human being on this planet.

The important point here is that you cannot imagine being able to feel that what is being done to other people is also being done to yourself. Obviously, this is one of the major causes of all conflict, but let us put that aside for now.

I would like to focus on the question of what it would take for a human being to be able to feel the suffering of others? What would it take for you to realize that when you hurt others, you are hurting yourself?

I would obviously have to have a different sense of awareness than I have right now.

That is an honest – and correct – answer. Almost every religion on this planet talks about the possibility that human beings can ascend to a higher realm and reach a state of immortality. Most religions also state that there are a number of immortal beings in this higher realm—however they choose to describe this realm. Now, could you see beings in a higher realm engage in the same kinds of conflicts and petty squabbles in which human beings engage?

1 | Who Would Start a Religious War?

No. I have always thought that in the spiritual realm there could not be the wars and other human atrocities we see on earth.

If there are no religious wars in heaven, it follows that before a human being can ascend to the spiritual realm, it somehow has to rise above human conflict, including religious conflict. How did we, who have already ascended to the spiritual realm, rise above human conflict?

In your current state of consciousness, in your current sense of awareness, you cannot see how to overcome conflict. The reason is that you do not feel a sense of oneness with other people; you feel separated from others. This is not a matter of simply putting more knowledge into your mental box. It is a matter of expanding your mental box so you can see what you cannot see right now.

Before you can ascend to the spiritual realm, you have to transcend your current state of consciousness, meaning that you have to overcome the sense of separation. You need to rise to a state of consciousness in which you feel one with all life, and therefore you realize that what is done to other human beings is also done to you. When you harm another human being, you are actually harming yourself, and that is the real reason you should do onto others what you want them to do to you. This statement of mine was not some imperial command given by a hellfire and brimstone preacher. I was simply pointing out what is enlightened self-interest, "enlightened" being the operative word.

I understand that, but how does it relate to my question about how you feel about people being killed in your name?

As an ascended being, I have attained a sense of oneness with all life. Any time a human being is killed, I consider it a tragedy. Every human being is one of my brothers or sisters. The person was alive because God wanted that lifestream to have the opportunity to be in embodiment on earth. When a person is killed, the opportunity is wasted, and that is a loss, not only for the individual but for the whole. Because I see myself as one with that whole, it is also a loss for me. It is always a loss for me when a person is killed. It makes no difference whether the person was killed for this or that reason. The loss is always immeasurable because each lifestream is a unique individual and each life represents a unique opportunity.

All killing is wrong in the eyes of God. That is why virtually every spiritual teaching on this planet denounces the killing of human beings. As a spiritual being, I do not discriminate based on human opinions and judgments. In reality, by assuming that I would feel differently based on why someone was killed, you are implying that some forms of killing are worse than others.

The logical consequence of that line of reasoning is that some forms of killing are not as bad. When you reason like that, it is only a matter of degree before you start believing that under certain circumstances killing is acceptable. The brutal fact is that the very moment you believe that under certain circumstances killing is an acceptable way to resolve human conflict, at that moment you have set the stage for religious war—and any other type of war for that matter. Do you see my point?

I do, and I am embarrassed that I didn't see that before.

There is no need to be embarrassed when you realize that you had a limited understanding. On the contrary, admitting that you have a limited understanding opens your mind to a higher understanding, and that is the driving force behind all human progress. What is truly embarrassing – and tragic – is when human beings refuse to admit that they have a limited understanding, and therefore they refuse to reach for a higher understanding. This is another major cause of religious conflict.

Now let us move on to your next assumption. You were assuming that people have actually been killed by Christians and that they have been killed in my name...

But this is not an assumption—it is simply historical fact!

Is it? How do you define a Christian?

Obviously it is a person who is a member of a Christian church.

I thought that was the problem. You are resorting to the common human tendency of defending one assumption by using another assumption—which easily leads people to build an entire belief system that is based exclusively on assumptions and has no bearing in truth. You are making the assumption that by becoming a member of a church that bears my name, a person will automatically become one of my followers. This is one of the most common mistakes made by both religious and nonreligious people. Religious people think that by obtaining membership in a particular religion, they have bought their salvation. Nonreligious people think they can blame the actions of the so-called followers on the founder of the religion. Everything done by so-called Christians is supposedly my fault, and if only I had stayed away from this planet, humankind would have been engaged in a group hug for the past 2,000 years.

I will agree that even if you had not come to earth, people would have found plenty of other things to fight about.

They would, but that obviously is no excuse for killing someone in the name of Christianity. Let us consider how a religion based on the principle of turning the other cheek became violent. Let me begin by pointing out that there are several thousand individual Christian churches and sects. They have vastly different doctrines and interpretations of the spiritual teachings they believe I gave. In many cases, these doctrines and interpretations are mutually exclusive, and many of the people you call Christians seriously believe that all other so-called Christians are not true believers and will go to hell. I assume you have observed this phenomenon?

I have, and it always shocked me a bit. I can understand some atheists or agnostics who reason that since so many Christian churches have opposing doctrines, they couldn't all be right so maybe none of them are right.

That is not necessarily an unworkable hypothesis, as long as you don't make the assumption that there is no higher truth that could take you beyond the conflicts between Christian churches. When you look at the conflicts between Christian churches, you realize that it isn't quite that simple to define what it means to be a Christian. You can't simply say that any member of any Christian church is a Christian.

You could reason that there can be only one true way to interpret the teachings I gave so therefore there must be one

1 | Who Would Start a Religious War?

true church. All the other churches are wrong and their members will go to hell. Which church do you pick as the only true one and how do you convince everybody else that your pick is the only right one? People have been taking this exclusivist approach for 2,000 years, and it hasn't resolved the conflicts. It has led to virtually all of the wars you mentioned earlier. Maybe we should look for a better approach?

Maybe there is a higher understanding of what it means to be a Christian? Maybe becoming a member of an outer church isn't enough to make you a true Christian? Maybe we could say that a true Christian is a person who is on the way to fully understanding and internalizing the true teachings of Christ, even to the point of living those teachings in every aspect of his or her life. The person is not just a Christian on Sunday mornings, but the person is living my true teachings 24/7/365.

That sounds reasonable. Does that mean that, according to your definition, no true Christian has ever killed another human being?

Not necessarily. Planet earth is a rather treacherous environment, and even true Christians can sometimes find themselves in situations where accidents happen. No true Christian ever killed another human being and felt that the killing was justified by my teachings. No true Christian ever killed someone in the name of Jesus Christ or in the name of God.

That sounds like a sensible definition. Do you mean that if a person has truly embodied your teachings that person would never use your teachings to justify killing another human being?

That is correct. How could they? Look at just a few of my statements:

> 38 Ye have heard that it hath been said, An eye for an eye, and a tooth for a tooth:
> 39 But I say unto you, That ye resist not evil: but whosoever shall smite thee on thy right cheek, turn to him the other also.
> 43 Ye have heard that it hath been said, Thou shalt love thy neighbour, and hate thine enemy.
> 44 But I say unto you, Love your enemies, bless them that curse you, do good to them that hate you, and pray for them which despitefully use you, and persecute you;
> 45 That ye may be the children of your Father which is in heaven: for he maketh his sun to rise on the evil and on the good, and sendeth rain on the just and on the unjust.
> 46 For if ye love them which love you, what reward have ye? do not even the publicans the same?
> 47 And if ye salute your brethren only, what do ye more than others? Do not even the publicans so?
> 48 Be ye therefore perfect, even as your Father which is in heaven is perfect. (Matthew, Chapter 5)

> And he answering said, Thou shalt love the Lord thy God with all thy heart, and with all thy soul, and with all thy strength, and with all thy mind; and thy neighbour as thyself. (Luke 10:27)

> 21 Then came Peter to him, and said, Lord, how oft shall my brother sin against me, and I forgive him? till seven times?

22 Jesus saith unto him, I say not unto thee, Until seven times: but, Until seventy times seven. (Matthew, Chapter 18)

These few statements present an approach to life that is completely nonviolent. How can you possibly love your neighbor as yourself? You can do so only when you realize that your neighbor is not separated from you. Your neighbor is part of a larger whole, namely the Body of God on earth, and you are also part of that whole. If you kill your neighbor, you are actually hurting yourself, as hurting a finger will affect the entire body.

My mission and teachings were meant to demonstrate that the true key to salvation is to move out of a state of consciousness that is dominated by a sense of separation and fear and move into a state of consciousness that is entirely based on a sense of oneness and love. I was telling people to stop responding to life with fear and to start responding with love. It is fear that makes people kill one another. Love is the only thing that can stop killing because perfect love casts out all fear (1John 4:18).

How do we then stop religious wars? I mean, a lot of wars were started by people who believed it was their holy duty to turn everyone into Christians, but I assume you are not going to say that we just have to turn everyone into true Christians?

Not necessarily, although that certainly would stop religious wars. A more realistic goal would be to help people become true followers of any true religion. A true Buddhist would never kill another human being, and neither would a true Muslim.

You mean that the cause of religious conflict is that people don't internalize the teachings of their particular religion?

Not exactly, although you are close. There are millions of people who count themselves as Christians and who have not fully internalized my teachings. They are striving to do so, and they have internalized enough of my teachings that they would never kill somebody in my name. These people have actually internalized a part of my teachings, and therefore they deserve to be called true followers. However, they are still following, meaning that they have not yet arrived at the destination of fully internalizing my teachings. In contrast, the people who start and reinforce religious conflicts have these characteristics:

- They firmly believe they have completely understood the teachings of their particular religion, and they are unwilling to consider any evidence to the contrary.

- They base this self-image on the fact that they believe the letter of their scriptures and follow the outer rules defined by their religion.

- Based on their interpretation of the outer letter, they firmly believe it is necessary and justified to use force to expand their religion. They believe their religion must replace all other religions. The more moderate people would not necessarily kill nonbelievers, but the more extremist people have no compunctions about killing in the name of God. All of these people believe that the greater purpose of doing God's work can justify a violation of God's laws, including my command to turn the other cheek or God's command not to kill.

Such people believe they know better than anyone else how their religious teachings should be interpreted. In reality, some of them even believe they know better than God. This is nothing but pride, and such intellectual and spiritual pride has the effect of making people blind. Neither God nor man can reach through these people's prideful beliefs and help these lifestreams see that they are trapped behind a wall of illusions. These people have set themselves outside the reach of truth and reason.

If you read the scriptures, you will see that I constantly challenged such people, and there was one particular word I used to characterize their approach to religion. There are over a dozen passages in the gospels in which I address the scribes and Pharisees and call them "hypocrites." I also made the following statement:

> For they bind heavy burdens and grievous to be borne, and lay them on men's shoulders; but they themselves will not move them with one of their fingers. (Matthew 23:4)

Most of the people who start religious conflicts sit in their temples of power and incite the general population to violence. They themselves avoid getting their hands dirty or running any risk of being killed.

Are all those who start religious conflicts hypocrites?

That is right, but what is the one thing that causes a person to act as a hypocrite? It is that the person believes in a lie and refuses to admit that it is a lie.

Virtually every religion known to man has scriptures that clearly and unconditionally denounce killing. Take for example the commandment: "Thou shalt not kill" (Exodus 20:13). Do you see any qualifications in that commandment? Do you see the scriptures define any conditions under which killing becomes acceptable?

No, but many people interpret other scriptural passages to mean that killing is acceptable.

Sure they do, but that is because they are imposing an interpretation that allows them so set aside the unconditional command that clearly says: "Thou shalt not kill!"

Look at the irony. We have three major religions that all honor the Old Testament, yet these three religions are among the most violent religions the world has seen. How can this be? If the followers of these religions had truly internalized and lived by the ten commandments, how could those followers have gone to war with each other? How could you have had the Crusades where Christians and Muslims killed each other and felt the killing was justified by the same God?

There can be only one reason, namely that people have found a way to neutralize, to nullify, the unconditional nature of the commandment not to kill. They have imposed a human interpretation upon the Word of God that makes God's word conditional and relative to the situation of human beings. When they have a neighbor who is too different, it suddenly becomes acceptable in the eyes of the priesthood to kill that neighbor.

This is the essence of hypocrisy, and it violates the first two commandments. The first one is: "Thou shalt have no other gods before me" (Exodus 20:3), and the meaning is clear. You cannot allow any man-made "god," any man-made idol, to stand between you and the real God. The real God is a God of love, not a God of war. When you interpret God's words to justify killing, or when you ignore God's words, you are violating the second commandment: "Thou shalt not make unto thee any graven image" (Exodus 20:4). When you take the unconditional statement "Thou shalt not kill" and cover it over with human conditions, then you have created a graven image. You are dancing around that golden calf instead of worshiping the true God who defined killing as unconditionally wrong.

2 | MORE THAN ONE TRUE RELIGION?

I am surprised to hear you say that there is more than one true religion. I think most people on this planet think of Christianity as an exclusivist religion. I know a lot of Christians who firmly believe that Christianity is the only true religion, and they act accordingly. They believe you commanded them to go into the world and turn all people into your disciples. They think you said that being a Christian is the only way to salvation, and they use your own statements to prove it. Here are the statements used most commonly to "prove" that Christianity is the only true religion:

> 15 And he said unto them, Go ye into all the world, and preach the gospel to every creature.
> 16 He that believeth and is baptized shall be saved; but he that believeth not shall be damned. (Mark, Chapter 16)

Jesus saith unto him, I am the way, the truth, and the life: no man cometh unto the Father, but by me. (John 14:6)

In the past many Christians – I mean members of Christian churches – have used those two statements to justify killing other people in your name. I think some of them even thought that it was better for people to be killed in the name of Christ than to go to hell.

It is very true that Christians have misinterpreted those and many other statements, using them as justification for turning a love-based spiritual movement into a fear-based religion. Nevertheless, where in these two statements does it say that in order to convert people to Christianity, it is acceptable to kill them?

Nowhere. Nevertheless, since these statements have obviously caused a lot of conflict, I think it is valid to ask what your true intention was behind those statements?

I did intend for true Christians to go into the world and preach my gospel to all creatures, but I did not mean the written gospels that are found in today's Christian Bible. As an aside, you might consider why I did not write down my teachings while I was alive? Could it be that I didn't want my disciples to preach from a written gospel but preach the Living Word given to them by the power of the Holy Spirit?

In reality, it was never my intention to convert everyone to a particular outer religion. It is known by scholars that my early followers were not called Christians. They were called

"Followers of the Way," and the reason was that I did not come to start a new religion.

That's in complete contradiction to everything I was told growing up!

Sure it is. That is because history is written by the winners. In this case, the winners were those who *did* turn my teachings into a fear-based religion and who *did* use that religion as a tool for gaining power over the population by controlling them through the fear of hell.

Nevertheless, I did not come to start a formal religion. Why do you think I was in constant opposition to the leaders of the Jewish religion? Just read the scriptures and see how I constantly challenged the scribes, the Pharisees, the lawyers, the Sadducees and the temple priests. Why do you think I challenged these people?

I guess you came to bring a new message, and they resisted that message.

That is true, and why did they resist it? They resisted it because they realized that my message was the ultimate threat to their position as a privileged elite who exercised almost total control over the population. They were not willing to give up their power or their privileges so they attempted to silence the voice that challenged their power over the people.

The power elite of the Jewish religion had almost total control over the people, and the basis for that control was the belief that the only key to the salvation of people's souls was the outer religion. Only those who believed the doctrines and obeyed the rules of the outer religion – the letter of the law – would go to heaven. Everyone else would go to hell.

The essence of this entire religious culture was that in order to be saved, you needed something from outside yourself. You are separated from heaven, from God, and in order to enter heaven, you have to go through a door. The Jews believed the door was located outside themselves. It was located in the Jewish temple, and the gatekeepers were the people controlling the outer religion. The leaders of the outer religion actually had the power to keep people out of heaven.

I challenged the very core of this religious culture, and my challenge can be summed up in two simple statements, the significance of which has been overlooked by most people, even those who claim to be Christians. The first statement is:

> Woe unto you, lawyers! for ye have taken away the key of knowledge: ye entered not in yourselves, and them that were entering in ye hindered. (Luke 11:52)

I earlier explained the nature of the key of knowledge. The key of knowledge is the fact that in order to enter the spiritual realm, you have to rise above the state of consciousness that is dominated by separation and fear. Instead, you have to attain a state of consciousness that is dominated by love and a sense of oneness with your source, with God. One might say that the true purpose of all true religion is to help people attain this shift in consciousness. Even though such a shift in consciousness can be facilitated by an outer religion, no outer religion can guarantee this shift. You cannot attain a higher state of consciousness by mechanically believing the doctrines of an outer religion and by blindly following all of its rules and rituals. The outer religion can help you discover the key of knowledge, but the key of knowledge is not found in, or confined to, the outer religion. Where is the key of knowledge to be found? I revealed that in another crucial statement:

2 | More than One True Religion?

> 20 And when he was demanded of the Pharisees, when the kingdom of God should come, he answered them and said, The kingdom of God cometh not with observation:
> 21 Neither shall they say, Lo here! or, lo there! for, behold, the kingdom of God is within you. (Luke, Chapter 17)

In today's world, most people overlook the significance of this statement, and they fail to understand that this single statement was the main reason the power elite of the established religion killed me. The significance of my statement is that the key to salvation, the doorway to the spiritual realm, is not the outer religion. The doorway to the spiritual realm is located inside yourself because the doorway is your mind, your consciousness. The only way to enter the spiritual realm is to rise to a higher level of consciousness.

One of the main purposes behind my mission was to demonstrate this higher state of consciousness. The many miracles I performed were direct results of having attained this state of consciousness. Contrary to the current idolatrous image of Jesus Christ, this state of consciousness was not exclusive to me. If I had been the only one who could attain this higher state of consciousness, what would have been the purpose for my coming to earth? I came more than anything to be an example, to demonstrate a path that all human beings have the potential to follow. That is why I said:

> Verily, verily, I say unto you, He that believeth on me, the works that I do shall he do also; and greater works than these shall he do; because I go unto my Father. (John 14:12)

How can you do the works that I did? Most people would say there is no way they could walk on water, and they are right. In their current state of consciousness, they cannot walk on water. In order to perform such seeming miracles, they would have to raise their state of consciousness. How do you attain a higher state of consciousness? Paul knew, and that is why he said:

> Let this mind be in you, which was also in Christ Jesus. (Philippians 2:5)

The basic fact behind all true religion is that there is a higher mind, a higher state of consciousness, a higher state of Being. Almost all religions portray – in one form or another – the fact that human beings have "fallen." In reality, this fall is a symbol for the descent into a lower state of consciousness. In this lower state of consciousness, people see themselves as separated from their source, and this sense of separation gives rise to fear. From this state of fear springs all of the negative human thoughts, feelings and actions, including religious wars and the need to feel that "my dad is stronger than your dad and my religion is better than your religion."

The ultimate solution to the problem of religious wars is that people must rise above the dualistic state of mind. They must attain a state of consciousness in which they see themselves as connected to their source. The key to overcoming the sense of separation is to attain what I called the Christ consciousness. I realize that after 2,000 years of Christians seeking to force their doctrines upon everyone, the term "Christ" is no longer universal. It was originally a universal term, but in today's world it might be prudent to say higher consciousness instead. Nevertheless, in this context we need to use the term Christ consciousness because it explains the two quotes that started this discussion. When I told my early followers to preach the gospel to every creature, I did not mean the written gospels. You might take note that at the time I made my statements, there *were* no written gospels since they were written down almost a lifetime later. I wanted my disciples to preach the gospel that there is a way out of the human dilemma, the human consciousness. The way out is to attain the mind of Christ whereby you move from a fear-based approach to life into a love-based approach. You move out of separation, which generates fear, and into union, which opens you to the perfect love that casts out all fear (1John 4:18).

It was my goal to lead all people out of the dualistic state of consciousness. This is what Paul called the carnal mind, and in Buddhism it has been called ignorance, Maya, or illusion. Other religions have other names. The name I used has unfortunately been misinterpreted, as so much else I said. My term for the dualistic state of consciousness was "death," meaning a state of being spiritually dead.

My true message is that as long as you are trapped in the death consciousness, dominated by separation from your source, you are spiritually dead. The only way to escape this death is to partake of the source of life, which is the Christ consciousness. In order to do that, you need to be baptized with spiritual fire, and that is why those who reject this fiery baptism will be damned. This does not mean that they will be punished by God. It means that they will remain in the death consciousness and thereby they punish themselves. They cannot enter into the state of union with the whole, and they will continue to suffer the effects of separation and fear.

The very source of life is the Christ consciousness. I came to demonstrate the way that leads to Christ consciousness, and in order to do that, I first had to walk that path. I had to become one with the Christ mind, and it was in this state of oneness that I made the statement: "I am the way, the truth, and the life." It does not mean that the outer person of Jesus is the only way to salvation. It means that the mind of Christ is the only way to salvation. Without allowing the mind of Christ to be in you, you cannot come to the Father, you cannot attain oneness with your source.

In order to receive spiritual life, you have to partake of the Christ consciousness. You have to partake of my "flesh and blood," and that is why I said:

> Verily, verily, I say unto you, Except ye eat the flesh of the Son of man, and drink his blood, ye have no life in you. (John 6:53)

Again, this statement has been misunderstood. You might have read that in the first centuries Christians were often accused of practicing cannibalism. Obviously, I never encouraged cannibalism so the only logical interpretation is that this statement has a deeper meaning. You are not eating physical flesh and drinking actual blood. You are taking in the spiritual substance of the mind of Christ, and this substance will then form a leaven that will raise your entire consciousness:

> Another parable spake he unto them; The kingdom of heaven is like unto leaven, which a woman took, and hid in three measures of meal, till the whole was leavened. (Matthew 13:33)

These statements were never meant to be interpreted as saying that the outer religion of Christianity is the only true religion or the only road to salvation. The true road to salvation is to follow the way, the inner path, whereby you put on the mind of Christ. In reality, members of any religion can follow

2 | More than One True Religion?

that path, and it does not matter that they call it something else. I wanted my followers to preach the gospel about the way to a higher state of consciousness, a way that transcends all outer religions. The last thing I wanted was for my followers to create another religion to compete with the existing religions because I knew such a religion would become as rigid and dogmatic as the religion that rejected me. Thereby, a Christian religion would inevitably become a tool in the ongoing human power struggle. It was inevitable that a power elite would form, and they would use the Christian religion to attempt to control the population. They would do this by perverting my teachings and once again take away the key of knowledge, namely that the doorway to the spiritual realm is found in your mind and that the key to salvation is a higher state of consciousness.

You have just blown away basically everything I was told about Christianity as I was growing up. You are being very direct.

That is right. I am a direct Master. I was never one to beat around the bush. That is why people said about me:

> And they were astonished at his doctrine: for he taught them as one that had authority, and not as the scribes. (Mark 1:22)

> The officers answered, Never man spake like this man. (John 7:46)

You might remember that I said:

> Think not that I am come to send peace on earth: I came not to send peace, but a sword. (Matthew 10:34)

The sword I came to bring is the sword of truth – the Sacred **WORD** of truth – that cleaves the real from the unreal. It all comes down to what I asked you earlier: "Do you want your present opinions confirmed, or do you want a higher understanding?" Most people do not want the truth, and that is why I so often said: "Those who have ears have better hear!"

Many people have the impression that you were a soft-spoken and loving teacher who welcomed and accepted everyone.

I am well aware of that, but where did they get that impression? Surely, it could not have come from an unbiased reading of the scriptures because they record many instances in which I challenged the scribes, the Pharisees and anyone else who promoted a fear-based approach to religion. I was a very loving teacher, but only in the sense that my love would not leave people trapped in their illusions. When necessary, I would challenge people's illusions in an attempt to awaken the lifestream and set it free. This is what people in today's world call "tough love," and I practiced it often, even toward my own disciples.

The simple fact is that many Christians have created an image of me that portrays me the way they want me to be, namely as a spiritual teacher who will not disturb them in their sense of comfortability. This idol obscures the truth that, as a spiritual teacher, it is my God-given role to disturb people and shake them out of their comfort zone. It is my role to challenge people's limited beliefs and help them see beyond those beliefs. It is my role to challenge their state of spiritual death and awaken their lifestreams to the eternal life of the Christ consciousness.

Those who persecuted and executed me were the people who were not willing to be disturbed. They were willing to kill the one sent by God in order to maintain the belief system in which they were comfortable. Sadly, many modern Christians have used my own teachings to create another belief system in which they are comfortable. It is precisely the refusal of these Christians to look beyond their comfortable beliefs that is responsible for many of the religious conflicts in today's world. Obviously, many other religious people are equally unwilling to leave their comfort zones. It is only people who are willing to look beyond their existing beliefs who can stop religious conflict.

Everything you said about the inner meaning of your statements and your true mission makes sense. But it is also in complete opposition to what most mainstream Christians have been brought up to believe, and I think we have lost any chance of orthodox Christians accepting this book.

What chance do you think there is that orthodox Christians will accept a book in which you claim to be speaking with the real Jesus?

Touché. But I still think we need to clarify the concept that there is more than one true religion. So many people from every religion have been brought up to believe that their religion is the only true one. Wouldn't you agree that the belief that there can be only one true religion is at the very core of religious conflict?

I agree. The concept that there can be only one true religion is one of the primary justifications used by the hypocrites to start religious conflicts. This belief is based on a complete misunderstanding of the purpose of religion. The hypocrites are completely blinded by their pride, and that is why they simply cannot understand the true purpose of religion. As I have just attempted to explain, the true purpose of religion is to help you attain a higher state of consciousness. That is why *a religion cannot save you.*

3 | THE TRUE PURPOSE OF RELIGION

The claim made by every religion I know of is that if you follow that religion to the letter, your salvation is guaranteed. How could a religion attract or retain followers if it didn't make that promise?

It could do so by giving people the truth about salvation. Many people are not able or willing to accept that truth, but in today's age an ever-increasing number of people are becoming ready to accept the truth about salvation. They would rather have the truth than empty promises, and they are able to tell the difference. When you do understand the truth about salvation, you clearly see why an outer religion or an outer savior cannot save you.

You know from the scriptures that when I walked the earth 2,000 years ago, I met thousands of people. They heard me teach, they saw me perform miracles of various kinds, yet many of them ignored or rejected me. Some even thought I was of the devil and that it was their holy duty to kill me in order to save the people from my deceit.

How was it possible that people could reject me and thereby reject their salvation?

Many modern Christians have been brought up to believe I was – or am – the only Son of God and the only Savior of humankind. Let us go with that thought and look at the logical consequence. Here I am, supposedly the only Son of God and the only Savior, and I have come to earth to save every lifestream. How come it was possible for people to reject me and thereby supposedly miss the boat that could take them to the shores of salvation? How come I was not able to save every lifestream? Why hasn't the kingdom of God, that I talked about many times, appeared on earth? If God truly is almighty, as most religions claim, why was it necessary for God to send me into the world as a savior? If God is ultimately in control, it must mean that God created the conditions that make it necessary for people to be saved. If God created everything, God must have created human beings as sinners.

Many Christians believe we are sinners by nature.

I am aware of that, but these people are not seeing that this would contradict the story of Adam and Eve. Clearly, before Adam and Eve ate the forbidden fruit, they were not sinners. They walked and talked with God, meaning that they were in a state of consciousness where they had some sense of connection to God. God has not created lifestreams to be sinners by nature. God has created them with the option to sin, but that does not necessarily mean that a lifestream *must* or *will* sin. If God created people's misery in the first place, why wouldn't God simply remove that misery by using the same power that created it? Simply put the video tape on rewind or push the undo button on the cosmic computer. Why go through the trouble of sending the only begotten Son and running the risk that some people might reject him and thereby miss their salvation?

> **Perhaps the fact that some people will miss their salvation means that God really is the angry and judgmental God it is portrayed to be, especially in the Old Testament? Maybe God doesn't want to save some people? They have offended God so it wants them to burn forever in hell.**

Many people have reasoned that way, but I was hoping you might see that this reasoning is illogical.

> **You are talking about the fact that God sent you to save us and that people can reject you, which means that God is not ultimately in control of who is saved and who isn't?**

Of course. The very fact that people have the ability to reject their salvation means that God is not the one deciding who is saved and who is not.

> **That sounds logical, but that is also against what most people think, including most Christians.**

Sure, but what they think is illogical. First of all, look at the following quote:

> For the Father judgeth no man, but hath committed all judgment unto the Son. (John 5:22)

If you are a Christian, you must reason that God is not deciding who is saved and who is not. God has put the Son in the judgment seat. How does the Son judge who is saved and who isn't? Is the Son deciding this arbitrarily? Is the Son judging based on the opinions of human beings or institutions? Or does the Son have some criteria that is above and beyond all human opinions?

The key to answering this question is to understand the nature of the Son of God. As I attempted to explain earlier, the only begotten Son of God is *not* the person of Jesus Christ. It is the universal Christ consciousness. Here is how it is determined who is saved and who is not. Those who rise above the consciousness of duality and attain the mind of Christ will attain a sense of oneness with their source. It is this sense of oneness that allows them to enter the kingdom of heaven and thereby be saved.

If you are still trapped in duality, you cannot enter the spiritual realm. Only those who have attained the Christ consciousness can enter the spiritual realm, and that is how the Son, meaning the mind of Christ, is judging who will enter the spiritual realm and who will remain on earth. This is explained between the lines in my parable about the wedding feast. One person entered the feast without wearing a wedding garment, which is a symbol for the Christ consciousness. He could not remain at the feast but was cast into outer darkness, which is a symbol for the dualistic state of consciousness (Matthew 22:11-12). Remember that I said the kingdom of God is within you, and the reason is that the kingdom of God is the Christ consciousness. When you attain the Christ consciousness, you are literally in the kingdom of God, even if you are still in a physical body on planet earth.

Again, you are making a lot of sense, but you are also contradicting everything most Christians were taught in Sunday school.

3 | The True Purpose of Religion

They were taught in Sunday school that Adam and Eve were cast out of paradise because they ate the forbidden fruit. Clearly, they made the choice to eat that fruit. People were never taught to consider what it really means that they had the option to eat the forbidden fruit.

The story of Adam and Eve demonstrates that although God is almighty, it has chosen to suspend its almighty power here on earth. God has chosen to set aside – at least temporarily – its power by giving human beings free will. God did not want to create a race of robots who were blindly following its laws. God wanted to create a race of self-conscious beings who were following its laws because they understood those laws. They could see that these laws did not restrict their freedom and creative expression. Instead, God's laws allow you to multiply your talents and take dominion over the earth without destroying yourself or the earth in the process. God wanted human beings to follow its laws based on the understanding that doing so is enlightened self-interest. Violating God's laws leads to self-destruction but following those laws leads to the abundant and eternal life.

When you have this understanding, you can choose to follow God's laws out of love instead of out of fear. In order to give you the option to choose out of love, God also had to give you the option to disobey its laws. Otherwise you would be a robot and not a self-conscious being.

When God decided to give you free will, it was inevitable that you also received the option to disobey its laws. God didn't want you to do so, but if you couldn't do so, how could you have the option to choose out of love? The problem is that if you do choose to go against God's laws, you will inevitably separate yourself from God. This separation will exist only in your mind, but as long as you choose to maintain it, you will see yourself as a mortal human being instead of the spiritual being that God created. Have you ever considered what the "fruit of the knowledge of good and evil" really means?

Not really. I always realized the story of the Garden of Eden couldn't be taken literally, but I couldn't quite grasp the deeper meaning.

Why do you say the story cannot be taken literally?

My mother told me she realized as a child that the Bible says Adam and Eve were the first people, meaning the only people. They had only three children and they were all sons. Obviously, those three sons couldn't produce children so how could we all descend from three men? My mother used this to reject all religion, but I never went that far. I just reasoned that there had to be a deeper understanding that I would find some day. What is that understanding?

That was a clever observation by your mother, and I understand why she used it to reject religion. However, I wish she would have taken your approach instead. It is always wise to assume that there could be an explanation that would resolve the seeming contradiction. This attitude makes it so much easier for you to grow than when you reject the possibility that a higher understanding might exist.

In this case, the solution is to realize that the story of Adam and Eve is meant to be a symbol, a metaphor, for what has happened to every lifestream. All people on earth have made the choice to eat of the forbidden fruit, however it was not an actual fruit but a state of consciousness. I earlier talked about the fact that all religions condemn killing so in order to kill in the name of God, people have to override that unconditional statement with conditions based on their own interpretations.

What has really happened here is that if a person is in alignment with the laws of God, then it would never kill another human being for any reason. The explanation being that when you are in alignment with the laws of God, you see yourself as part of the Body of God, and you realize all other people are also part of that Body. By killing another, you are only hurting yourself. You understood this principle, right?

I do, although I won't pretend that I can feel that sense of oneness. I understand it intellectually, I just don't feel I have fully internalized what you are saying.

An honest answer. But you understand it enough that you wouldn't kill anyone in my name?

Absolutely!

Good, then you are on your way to fully internalizing it. All lifestreams on earth have departed – to a greater or lesser degree – from that sense of oneness with their source. This means that they have "fallen" into a lower state of consciousness, and this is the state of consciousness that is illustrated in Genesis as the "fruit of the knowledge of good and evil."

When you have a sense of oneness with your source, you have an absolute standard for evaluating your behavior, what most people call "right and wrong." If you do something that is in alignment with God's laws, it will enhance all life, and therefore it is life-supporting. If you do something that violates God's laws, it will hurt yourself and all life. It is self-destructive, meaning that it is not enlightened self-interest. No sane person will hurt itself. You can hurt yourself only out of ignorance, the ignorance that springs from the consciousness of separation and duality.

Are you saying that when we lose our sense of being part of a larger whole, we become trapped in selfishness and think we can hurt others without affecting ourselves? When we become enlightened, we see that all people are part of the Body of God so by hurting another, we also hurt ourselves?

Exactly! When you separate yourself from God, you forget God's laws, even though God has put those laws in your inward parts (Jeremiah 31:33). This means that deep within you, you have the potential to know God's laws – you have the key of knowledge – but your outer mind has forgotten this. Your outer mind is trapped in a sense of separation, and this creates a state of duality in your mind. The consequence is that you can no longer evaluate right and wrong based on the absolute standard of God's law. You must create a new standard, but this standard will not be absolute. It will be a relative standard based on how you – or your culture, political system or religion – define good and evil.

How does God define good and evil? In reality, God has no such definitions because they are relative. Good is defined as the opposite of evil and vice versa. In God there are no opposites but only oneness. In God's mind, there is only one question: "Is it in alignment with my laws or is it out of alignment with my laws; is it life-supporting or self-destructive?" This is an absolute standard, and it has no room for "variableness, neither shadow of turning" (James 1:17). In the consciousness of duality, there is unlimited room for variableness. The consequence being that it is entirely possible that what human beings define as good is nevertheless out of alignment with God's law. For example, when some human beings define it as a virtue to kill nonbelievers, they are clearly out of alignment with God's Law of Love. They think they are doing good, but they are deceived by duality.

The forbidden fruit was the consciousness of duality in which people are trapped by the relative opposites of good and evil, meaning that they have lost contact with God's law. This loss of an absolute standard is what allows people to create their own, self-centered, definitions of good and evil. This is how people can circumvent the unconditional command "Thou shalt not kill." They simply use their relative definitions of good and evil to say that in some cases killing is not wrong. It is necessary to kill in order to promote the cause that they have defined as the greater good. They now believe that it is necessary to do evil that good may come. People in this state of consciousness actually believe that the goal of bringing God's kingdom to earth can justify that they violate God's laws.

That is a very enlightening thought. The real problem on earth is that we have lost the perception of God's law and this has caused us to create all of our problems. Now some people think that in order to get back to paradise, we have to violate God's law in order to overcome the violation of God's law. But in reality, the only way to get back to paradise is to bring ourselves back into alignment with God's law of oneness, and we can do that only by overcoming duality, meaning separation from our source.

Correct. It is like the old saying that two wrongs don't make a right. You cannot erase an error by committing another error; you simply have to rise above the state of consciousness that causes you to violate God's laws. One might say that you cannot solve a problem as long as you are trapped in the dualistic state of consciousness that created the problem in the first place.

That reminds me of the story of the Gordian knot. An ancient king had created a very intricate knot and an oracle had prophesied that the person who could "undo" the knot would become ruler over all of Asia. Many people tried to untie the knot, but none succeeded. Finally, Alexander the Great cut the knot in two with his sword. Instead of trying to reverse the process that created the knot, Alexander took an entirely different approach.

A good example of how you must transcend the consciousness that created the problem before you can see the obvious solution. The issue is that when people begin to create their own definitions of good and evil, they are suddenly able to justify virtually any act.

The real cause of religious conflict is that people have fallen into a lower state of consciousness that allows them to feel justified in violating the laws of God, even to the point of killing in the name of God. They use a relative interpretation of the doctrines of their particular religion to override God's commands. They take a definition that is actually relative and elevate it to the status of being absolute. They believe a man-made "law" is actually God's law. This is the ultimate illusion that is the start of all religious conflict, and for that matter all conflicts between people.

The irony is obvious. Religion was given to people to set them free from the duality consciousness. Some people use religion to anchor themselves even more firmly in that state of separation. They literally use religion to do the opposite of what God intends, yet they are firmly convinced they are doing God's work. This becomes a catch-22, and it is extremely difficult for a spiritual teacher to free people from this state of mind.

In reality, the only way to bring God's kingdom to earth – and the only way to win your personal salvation – is to bring your lifestream back into alignment – meaning oneness – with God's laws. Thereby, your outer mind can know the laws written in your inward parts, and only then can you choose to follow those laws out of love. The only way to truly know God's laws is through the only begotten Son of God, for as I said:

> All things are delivered unto me of my Father: and no man knoweth the Son, but the Father; neither knoweth any man the Father, save the Son, and he to whomsoever the Son will reveal him. (Matthew 11:27)

The true meaning is that you can know God and God's laws only through the Christ consciousness. When you are trapped in the consciousness of duality, you cannot see God's law; you see only a man-made interpretation, a graven image, that obscures the true law. My mission was meant to demonstrate that all people have the potential to put on the mind of Christ and thereby come back into alignment with their God and its laws.

That's a very profound explanation. I do have a follow-up question. The fruit of the knowledge of good and evil is a state of consciousness. This is a logical consequence of free will. When God gave us free will, God had to give us the possibility of separating ourselves from itself. When we do so, we automatically

descend into the consciousness of duality where good and evil become relative concepts. Correct?

You have understood the central point. If we could get all people to understand this point, we would be well on our way to ending religious conflict on this planet.

How does this tie into what we talked about earlier, namely that no outer religion or savior can save us?

The process of salvation is not a mechanical process. It is not a matter of blindly believing in a particular outer doctrine or blindly following an outer leader. Salvation is not a matter of a heavenly being – be it Jesus Christ, the Buddha, Krishna, Jehovah or Allah – who appears in the sky and sweeps you up into heaven. Many religions give their followers the impression that following the outer rules will automatically get them to heaven. This outer path to salvation is what the Bible describes in the following quote:

> There is a way which seemeth right unto a man, but the end thereof are the ways of death. (Proverbs 14:12)

I rebuked the belief in an outer road to salvation in the following statement:

> For I say unto you, That except your righteousness shall exceed the righteousness of the scribes and Pharisees, ye shall in no case enter into the kingdom of heaven. (Matthew 5:20)

Salvation is an artistic or mystical process because it depends on choices you make. You are saved when you attain a higher state of consciousness in which you no longer see yourself as separated from your source. No person or organization from outside yourself can make you put on the mind of Christ. You are the only one who can change your mind. You are the one who must decide to leave behind the old man of the dualistic consciousness and put on the new man of the Christ mind. Paul described this process when he said:

> 22 That ye put off concerning the former conversation the old man, which is corrupt according to the deceitful lusts;
> 23 And be renewed in the spirit of your mind;
> 24 And that ye put on the new man, which after God is created in righteousness and true holiness. (Ephesians, Chapter 4)

This is also the true meaning behind the concept that you have to be born again and become a new person in Christ. This was understood clearly by many of the early Christians, but when the orthodox church elevated me to the status of a God, they turned me into an idol. Today, most Christians use Christian doctrines to deny their potential to put on the mind of Christ. This denial of your own Christ potential – the denial of the Christ that rules in the kingdom of God within you – ties you to the consciousness of duality. The Christ mind allows you to feel one with your source, and the consciousness of duality creates separation. It follows that duality is the consciousness of anti-christ.

We have now arrived at the point where those who have ears to hear will be able to know the truth in their hearts, namely that the true purpose of religion is not to save you through some outer measure. The true purpose of religion is to empower you to save yourself by following a systematic path whereby you put off the dualistic consciousness and attain a higher state of consciousness based on union with your source, union with God in the inner kingdom.

We might say that the Garden of Eden was a schoolroom for lifestreams. They lived in a protected environment where they had constant access to a spiritual teacher who was teaching them how to attain Christ consciousness, meaning a sense of oneness with their source. Some lifestreams chose to turn their backs on this teacher, and they fell into the consciousness of duality. Lifestreams still have the opportunity to learn, and it is beneficial for all spiritually minded people to consider earth as a schoolroom.

There are two ways to learn in the schoolroom of earth. One is what we might call the School of Hard Knocks or the school of unconscious learning. People go through life without seeking any deeper understanding of the spiritual side of life, meaning that they are not striving to rise above the consciousness of duality. They can learn only by seeing the consequences of their actions, or as the Bible says:

> Be not deceived; God is not mocked: for whatsoever a man soweth, that shall he also reap. (Galatians 6:7

> Even science has confirmed that no one escapes the consequences of their actions, and it is called the law of action and reaction. Or as stated in the popular saying: "What goes around, comes around."

The purpose of true religion is to offer people an alternative to the School of Hard Knocks. Religion is meant to offer people a systematic path that allows them to rise above duality and attain the higher consciousness, the Christ consciousness. That is why my life was meant to demonstrate this path, as were the lives of other spiritual teachers sent to earth. When religion becomes perverted by the consciousness of duality, people begin to believe that the outer religion is the key to salvation, and that is when you have sown the seeds of religious conflict. You have sown the wind and will surely reap the whirlwind (Hosea 8:7).

Most Christians would vehemently deny that we can save ourselves. They will say that we are saved only through God's grace.

They are right, but they don't understand the concept of grace. You *are* saved only through God's grace, but what is God's grace? It is the fact that God has sent its Son into the world so that through him the world might be saved (John 3:17). But what is the only begotten Son? It is the Christ consciousness. How can you be saved through the Christ consciousness? You can do so only by putting on the mind of Christ, by becoming *one* with that mind.

God's grace is not automatically given to anyone based on outer criteria. I realize many Christians believe they can be saved by declaring Jesus Christ as their Lord and Savior, but it simply isn't true. I cannot save people against their free will. Everything in your life depends on the choices you make by exercising the free will given to you by God. In order to be saved by God's grace, you must make the free-will choice to accept God's grace. How can you receive God's grace? You can do so only by taking in God's grace, meaning the Christ consciousness, and allowing it to transform your consciousness. Once again, look at my statement:

> Another parable spake he unto them; The kingdom of heaven is like unto leaven, which a woman took, and hid

in three measures of meal, till the whole was leavened. (Matthew 13:33)

You must absorb a portion of the mind of Christ – which is God's grace – and allow it to raise your entire consciousness. Sadly, most mainstream Christians reject the grace of God and refuse to let this mind be in them which was also in me. They use certain interpretations of my own words to justify this rejection. Those interpretations were born of the consciousness of duality.

Do you mean that many religious doctrines are based on the consciousness of duality—what you call the consciousness of anti-christ? Most Christians believe the Bible is the infallible word of God, and many people from other religions say the same thing about their scriptures. Are you saying a religious scripture is not an absolute truth?

Absolutely! Nothing in this world is absolute, and if you think it is, you are fooling yourself. Albert Einstein proved that everything is relative. It is called the theory of relativity, and it is an excellent observation of one of the basic facts of life. But now that we have discussed the true purpose of religion, perhaps we should discuss the true purpose of religious scriptures?

4 | THE TRUE PURPOSE OF RELIGIOUS TEACHINGS

After telling me that it is not the purpose of religion to save us, you are now going to tell me that it is not the purpose of religious scripture to give us truth?

Define truth!

What?

Define what you mean by truth. Do you have a clear vision of what exactly you mean when you say "truth?"

It is something that is accurate, factual and can be verified.

What criteria do you use to define what is accurate and factual and how do you verify that something is true?

There is observation and common sense. For example, we all know that the earth is round. It

is something we can observe with our senses. It's just a fact we can verify.

I didn't realize you had been an astronaut.

What do you mean?

Have you traveled into space to see with your own eyes that the earth is round? If you haven't, how do you know? Up until 500 years ago, most people believed the earth was flat. That belief was based on their senses and they would have used your argument—everyone knows the earth is flat; it's obvious.

I am not trying to dispute that the earth is round but to point out that the human senses cannot necessarily tell you truth. There are many examples of how a common belief has been completely wrong. If you rely solely on the senses and common sense, you will not necessarily know truth.

Then there is scientific truth. We conduct a scientific experiment that proves our theory. For example, we have conducted many scientific experiments that prove atoms exist even though we can't see them with our senses.

If you studied science history, you would quickly discover that there have been several periods where scientists believed they had discovered the final theory about how the world was created. Only a few years later, their final "truth" was replaced by a new theory. Before Einstein, scientists believed the world was made of two elements, matter and energy. Einstein proved that matter is another form of energy. Today, scientists are working on theories that could make Einstein's findings obsolete. Even the existence of atoms is disputable. Sure there is some kind of phenomenon, but the latest theories have invalidated the model that most people were taught in school, namely that the atom is like a miniature solar system. The concept of an atom is simply a mental image projected upon the actual phenomenon. This has even been proven by quantum physics, which states that you cannot observe reality as it is because your state of consciousness influences your observation.

Yes, I am aware of the findings of quantum physics. Okay, then how about religious truth. A religious teaching was given by God, and therefore we can know truth by comparing an idea to the religious teaching, such as the Bible.

But if a religious truth was absolute, why have people come up with so many different interpretations of a given religious scripture? Why are there so many different Christian churches and sects?

Are you saying that a religious scripture is not necessarily an absolute truth even though it was given by God?

How can anything expressed in words be an absolute truth? How can anything in this world be absolute? How can a human being, trapped in the consciousness of separation and duality, ever know the absolute truth? Let me try to make this less abstract. Look at the first two of the ten commandments:

> 3 Thou shalt have no other gods before me.
> 4 Thou shalt not make unto thee any graven image.
> (Exodus, Chapter 20)

Why do you think God gave these two commandments as the very first ones?

Probably because they were the most important.

Good answer, so why were they the most important? What did I say was the key to salvation?

That we attain a higher state of consciousness in which we no longer see ourselves as separated from God.

Since God obviously knew the key to salvation, would it not seem reasonable that the first two commandments seek to instruct you in how to overcome the sense of separation from God? How can you get to feel a sense of union with God? You can do so only when you know the true God and do not worship some other god. How can you avoid worshiping a false god? By not creating a graven image, meaning an image that is based on the things of this world and the consciousness of duality.

Remember what I said about the consciousness of duality, namely that it prevents people from seeing absolute truth. It causes people to create a mental image of what they believe is truth; they *define* truth instead of *finding* truth. This is also what causes people to create a false image of God, and when they think their image gives a true and absolute portrayal of God, they will be trapped by their own image. If they think the image is the absolute truth and that God is confined to their image, they will never seek to look beyond it. They will never see the true God who is beyond any graven images that human beings could possibly create. God was well aware of this mechanism, and that is why the first two commandments were to never allow your view of God to be confined to an outer image—which includes any religious scripture or doctrine.

That is a very profound interpretation of the first two commandments. No religious scripture was ever meant to tell us the absolute truth about God?

Exactly. How could God possibly be confined to any description expressed in words? Consider the fact that words are relative. They are subject to different interpretations by different people, and the reason is that when people are in the consciousness of duality, they will interpret religious scriptures according to their own relative beliefs. They have created a mental image of God, and they seek to force that image upon the religious scripture. They are looking at the scripture through the filter of their relative image of God, and they are looking for things that will confirm their mental image. That is the real reason for the countless disputes among religious people concerning how to interpret religious scripture. It is also one of the key components in religious conflict.

That sounds true so what is the way out? How do we overcome this tendency to fight over which person or church has the "only true" interpretation of scripture?

By giving up the idea that your particular religious scripture is the only truth or an absolute truth!

I foresee that many people will find that difficult to accept.

Let me try to make this less abstract by asking you to pick up a Bible.

Okay, I am holding a Bible.

Now open the Bible and find God in the Bible.

What do you mean? Obviously God isn't in the actual book I am holding in my hand.

Why not?

Because God is the almighty. I mean, God created the entire universe so how could a God that created an almost infinitely big universe be confined to a book I can hold in my hand?

A good observation. I wish all people who revere the Bible would come to that realization because it might keep them from turning the Bible into a graven image that prevents them from seeing the God who is beyond the Bible—and any other religious scripture. If God is not in the Bible, then what is the Bible?

Many would say it is an accurate and true description of God.

But we just discussed the fact that the second commandment tells people not to take unto themselves a graven image. If the Bible describes God, that description must per definition be a graven image and therefore a violation of the second commandment. According to the definition held by many

Christians, if the Bible is a description of God, then the Bible is not biblical.

Many people need to change their view of the Bible. If they believe the Bible was given to humans by God, they need to realize that God will not violate its own commandments. God has not given the Bible for the purpose of providing a complete, absolute and unchangeable description of God, God's truth or God's law. God is well aware that words are ambiguous and that people who are trapped in the consciousness of duality can twist any religious scripture. Don't you think God realizes that the consciousness of duality can make its commandments relative whereby people can use God's own words to justify killing each other in the name of God?

The logical conclusion is that unless people think God was stupid, they need to consider the fact that God did not give the Bible for the reason they were told in Sunday school. God had no intention whatsoever of giving people an absolute truth because God realizes that any statement expressed in words is not truth but only an approximation of truth. People need to consider why God actually gave them the Bible and what its real intentions were. What does God want people to do with the Bible? Does God want you to turn it into a weapon to use against your fellow man, or does God want you to use it as a springboard for winning your salvation? Does God want you to turn it into an idol or does God want you to use it as a stepping stone for finding the Spirit of Truth that cannot be expressed in words?

That is a very thought-provoking idea. But let me first make sure I understand the concept that the Bible is not truth but only a description of truth. Could you elaborate on that?

Let me tell you a parable. There once was an expedition that penetrated deep into a dense jungle. On the way, the explorers passed a beautiful mountain, and one of them took a picture of the mountain that he developed and enlarged. After a few days, they came across a native tribe. No member of the tribe had ever ventured far from their village so to broaden their horizons, the explorer gave them the photo of the mountain. They asked him many questions about it, but due to the language barrier, he wasn't sure they actually understood his explanation.

Several generations later, another expedition came to the village. They noticed that the members of the tribe worshiped something on an altar. When they approached, they noticed the object of worship was an old black and white photograph.

After getting to know the tribe, the expedition members realized that the native people believed the photograph itself was an image of God. They had never seen another photograph nor had they seen a mountain so they simply did not understand the concept that the photograph depicted an actual thing here on earth. They believed they had been given their image by a god-man, who had visited their village a long time ago. The tribe believed the new expedition was a return of the god-man because they had so faithfully worshipped their god.

Because the expedition members were modern scientists, they felt uncomfortable about being revered as god-men and they felt obligated to lead these people out of their illusion. They promised to take the people to the kingdom of God and the entire tribe followed them. After a few days, the tribe arrived at the exact spot where the photograph was taken. Upon seeing the photograph and the mountain at the same time, the native people realized that the photograph was not an image of God but only a representation of an object on earth. Instantly, their world view crumbled. The scientists soon left,

4 | *The True Purpose of Religious Teachings*

feeling they had done their duty to the cause of truth by leading these people out of their illusion.

What is the message in this story? To a scientist the message is that there is no God and that all religious people worship illusions. To modern Christians the message is that the tribe was worshipping a false god, and they would have handed them a Bible instead. The real message is that even a religious scripture is just a description, as the photograph was a representation of the mountain. The photo was not the real thing, and likewise no religious scripture is the real truth. The Bible is not God or God's truth but only a representation of that truth expressed in words that human beings can understand. If you want to know truth, you have to look beyond the representation. If you do not look beyond the outer words, you turn the Bible into a graven image, and many well-meaning people have done just that. God's truth cannot be confined to any religious scripture because God's truth – God's Being – is beyond any words or images found in this world. That is why God does not want people to create a graven image and say that the image is the absolute truth. Doing so inevitably causes people to worship a false God of their own making. The reason is that God's truth cannot be known by the human senses, by science or by religion. That is why I said:

> God is a Spirit: and they that worship him must worship him in spirit and in truth. (John 4:24)

God's truth cannot be known through the dualistic mind. You simply cannot know God's truth as long as you see that truth as being outside of, separated from, yourself. You can know God's truth fully only when you merge with the Spirit of truth, when you become one with truth. At that moment, you will exclaim: "I am the way the truth and the life!" (John 14:6).

I have to be the pessimist and say I think this will leave most people feeling left out. I mean, how can we possibly hope to experience the oneness with truth you are talking about?

You can do this by coming to understand the true purpose behind religion and by applying that understanding. As I explained before, the central problem is that people are trapped in the consciousness of duality that prevents them from knowing truth. The only way out is to reach for the higher state of consciousness, namely the mind of Christ. The true purpose of religion is to provide people with a systematic path that gradually leads them out of duality and into the oneness of the Christ consciousness. We might call it the spiritual path, and it was the way I taught my disciples, which is why they were called "Followers of the Way."

The end goal is that you attain the full Christ consciousness that helps you overcome all sense of separation from God. Getting to that point is a gradual process whereby you gain a progressively deeper understanding of truth. What drives this progress is that you have direct experiences of truth. Truth cannot be known by the dualistic mind because to this mind everything is relative. Truth can be known only through a direct experience, what the Greeks and some of my early followers called gnosis—meaning that there is no separation between the knower and the known. It is only by experiencing truth directly that you are convinced there is something beyond the dualistic mind. It was never the true purpose of religious scriptures to give you an absolute truth. God never wanted you to confine your image of it to any religious scripture because a scripture is just a representation of the real thing, as the photo is not the mountain. God's intent behind giving people a religious scripture is to help them attain an inner experience of truth. This experience is another way to explain "the key of knowledge." The problem is that if people are completely trapped by duality, they will inevitably misunderstand God's intent. They will believe that since the scripture came from God, it must be an absolute truth. As a result, they cannot see beyond the outer scripture. They cannot fathom the idea that truth is not found in the scripture but that truth is found only by looking beyond the outer word. Truth can be known only by going beyond the outer description because truth must be found in the kingdom of God. As I have mentioned before, the kingdom of God is within you. An outer scripture is only meant to be a stepping stone for taking a leap of faith into the inner kingdom of direct experience. All human beings have the ability to experience truth directly, if only they will make a conscious effort to reach beyond the dualistic mind. Most people have had such experiences of truth, and they are often called "Aha" experiences or intuitive flashes.

But almost anyone has had those so most people must have experienced truth?

All people have had some experience of truth. It is important to realize that an intuitive experience doesn't necessarily give you an absolute truth. What it does give you is a direct experience of a level of reality that is beyond the dualistic state of mind. Many people are still so influenced by a belief system that springs from duality that they cannot have a clear intuitive experience or they cannot interpret the experience correctly. Paul knew this and that is why he said:

> For now we see through a glass, darkly; but then face to face: now I know in part; but then shall I know even as also I am known. (1Corinthians 13:12)

We might say that intuition is like a powerful telescope that allows you to probe the night sky beyond what is visible with the naked eye. All people have their personal telescope, but for some the lens might be covered with grease or dirt. If they will make an effort to clean the lens, meaning that they free their minds from dualistic beliefs and doctrines, all people can gradually gain a clearer view of truth. This is the only process that can truly lead people beyond the dualistic state of consciousness that causes all religious conflict.

Does this have any bearing on the old question of whether God exists? Many religious people believe in God but have no proof of God's existence. How could you possibly prove the existence of God?

There is only one way to prove the existence of God and that is through a direct, inner experience of God's Being. Because every lifestream was created in the image and likeness of God (Genesis 1:26), any person has the capacity of consciousness to experience God's essential Being. This is an experience that every human being can have by doing what it takes to achieve that experience.

You mean, if a person is truly spiritual, that person should strive for a direct experience of God?

Of course. How can you claim to be a spiritual person if you are not willing to experience the reality of what you believe? There is no substitute for direct experience. Religion was never meant to be a substitute for the experience of God. Why would a true spiritual teacher want people to settle for a description of God when they have the capacity of consciousness to attain a direct experience of God's Being?

5 | WHY SO MANY DIFFERENT RELIGIONS?

Your statement that we need to leave behind the idea that there is only one true religion brings up a question I have always been wondering about. If there is more than one true religion, then God must have given humankind more than one religious teaching. I understand the idea that a religious teaching is not meant to give us absolute truth, but I still think most people will wonder why God would give us religious teachings that are so different and in some cases seem to be contradictory. If we didn't have different religions, it would seem there would be less basis for religious conflict so why didn't God simply give us one religion?

Let me start with the last thought. We have already seen that people have used my teachings to develop many different churches and doctrines. Even if people start out with the same religious teaching, the dualistic state of mind will still lead to the development of different and contradictory doctrines. Even if there had been only one religion, people would still be fighting over religion. Now for the next point. To understand why there are different religions, it is helpful to consider where religious teachings actually come from. So far we have said that a religious teaching is given by God, but we can be a lot more specific. Since you keep bringing up how Christians reject anything not based on the Bible, let us begin by looking at an interesting passage:

> 28 And it came to pass about an eight days after these sayings, he took Peter and John and James, and went up into a mountain to pray.
> 29 And as he prayed, the fashion of his countenance was altered, and his raiment was white and glistering.
> 30 And, behold, there talked with him two men, which were Moses and Elias:
> 31 Who appeared in glory, and spake of his decease which he should accomplish at Jerusalem. (Luke, Chapter 9)

If you believe in the Bible, this passage clearly demonstrates the following:

• There are spiritual beings in a higher realm, and there must be many of them since the Book of Revelation talks about a multitude (Revelation 7:9).

• At least some of these beings have ascended from earth, meaning that they were once in a human body and have now ascended to heaven (Moses and Elias). One might call them ascended beings or ascended masters.

- Such ascended masters can appear to and interact with human beings.

- The ascended masters can act as teachers, tutoring those on earth.

I know some will say that I was so special, and that is why they appeared to me, but there are many examples in the Bible of how ascended masters and angels have appeared to people. You can find similar examples from virtually every religion. Even people who follow no outer religion have had such visitations or visions.

There is a large group of beings in the spiritual realm who serve as the spiritual teachers for humankind. Throughout the ages, we have been called by many names, but in this case, let us use the name "ascended masters" to indicate that we are ascended and that there are many of us. Our assignment from God is to save every lifestream on earth within the parameters of God's laws, which includes the Law of Free Will. We are not assigned to save people by doing all the work for them. We are assigned to give people the understanding and the tools that will empower them to save themselves.

The importance of this statement is that we never manipulate people or force anything upon them. We use only positive persuasion and seek to help people make the right choices by increasing their understanding. We are not seeking to force people into being saved. We are seeking to inspire them to use the free will given to them by God to choose salvation out of love. The conclusion being that when we give people a spiritual teaching, we have to adapt that teaching to people's current level of consciousness.

To illustrate this, let me compare our situation to a teacher who is standing in front of a class of kindergarten students. The teacher has a college degree and has a very advanced understanding of math, yet there is no way he could teach advanced math to children at the kindergarten stage. He holds back some of his knowledge and starts by teaching them the simple concept of addition. The teacher knows that you simply cannot teach the more advanced concepts to beginning students. You have to take a gradual approach, and as the students increase their understanding of the topic, you can give them a progressively more advanced teaching.

If you want to be critical, you could say that the teacher is deliberately deceiving the students. He knows there is a lot more to math than addition, but he is withholding that information to avoid overwhelming and discouraging them. Thereby, he is giving the students the incorrect impression that math is pretty simple and easy to learn. When the students have mastered addition, they could potentially develop the belief that they know everything they need to know about math. They might even refuse to learn any further teaching.

On the other hand, you have to recognize that the teacher is in a bind. If he taught college-level math to students in kindergarten, they would have no basis for understanding the teaching. They would likely give up, feeling that math was far beyond them. If you want to be realistic, you have to say that the teacher is taking the only practical approach. As long as he does not tell the students that addition is all they will ever need to know about math or stops teaching them more advanced concepts, he is doing the practical thing.

Of course, if the students develop the idea that addition is the only true form of math and therefore refuse to learn about multiplication, then you might have a problem. If the teacher was bound to respect the free will of the students, he might actually have to abandon the students, leaving them to go through life believing math offers nothing beyond addition. This example describes the situation faced by the ascended masters as we try to teach our unascended brothers and sisters about the spiritual side of life.

When we consider how to help a particular group of people raise their awareness of God, we have to consider their present beliefs, their culture and their level of consciousness. I am not hereby trying to say that you should attach any value judgment to this by saying that one group of people are better or more important than others. I am simply saying that people in different cultures need different religious teachings. As the spiritual teachers of humankind, we study this topic extensively. One might say that we have a far better foundation for determining which spiritual teaching will work best for a particular culture than do people who are still trapped in duality. Obviously, you have to add to this that as people do raise their consciousness, a religion will have to adapt. I have little sympathy for the millions of Christians who believe that Christianity doesn't need to change. The Western world has changed immensely over the past 2,000 years, and you can see this by comparing what the average person knows today to what the average person knew back then. It simply doesn't make any sense to ignore this fact or reason that it should have no effect on Christianity. Do modern Christians really think that if I walked the earth today, I would say exactly the same as I said 2,000 years ago? Do they think I would ignore the many problems people face in today's world, problems that were unknown 2,000 years ago? The brutal fact is that if Christianity does not adapt to the growth in people's consciousness, including some of the indisputable findings of science, it simply cannot meet people's spiritual needs in this age. Christianity is no different from any other religion in that it must either change or die.

You are saying that no religious teaching is meant to last forever. It is only when people don't apply the teaching that it will remain unchanged for a long period of time?

That is correct. If people understand the intention behind giving them a religious teaching, they will use it as a stepping stone for attaining direct experiences of truth. This will increase their understanding of the spiritual side of life, and the ascended masters can then give them a more advanced teaching. Again, the key of knowledge is not the outer teaching but a direct, inner experience of truth.

I think that will be a difficult concept for many people because so many religions promote the image that their religion gives the absolute truth. If a truth is absolute, it could never change or be expanded.

Yes, but that is an extremely arrogant and prideful idea. It is based on the assumption that the generation that received a given religious scripture had a high enough state of consciousness to receive God's absolute truth. It isn't hard to see that the people who received the Old Testament were in a much lower state of awareness than most modern people. It shouldn't be difficult to reason that these people simply weren't ready to receive God's highest truth, and they were given a teaching that was not the highest possible. Why do people think God sent me to give people a higher teaching than what is found in the Old Testament? The simple fact is that there are certain cycles in the spiritual life of humankind, and when a new cycle is initiated, God gives those who have ears to hear a new and higher teaching.

5 | Why so Many Different Religions?

Most people have never heard about the existence of such cycles. Why is it important to know about spiritual cycles?

It depends on your approach to religion. If you take the outer approach and think your religion is the only true one and that your scripture gives an absolute truth, you will have to reject the reality of spiritual cycles. If your doctrine is infallible, it could never change so no progress is possible. If you are a truly spiritual person, you will want to know about spiritual cycles because they are part of the forward movement of humankind. They are designed by the ascended masters to help people raise their consciousness.

Each spiritual cycle presents a unique opportunity for growth, but also a unique challenge. In order to make the best possible use of the current spiritual cycle, you have to learn the lesson from the previous cycle. Then you have to be willing to let go of at least some aspects of your old approach to religion. Those who – for various reasons – will not flow with the spiritual cycles, often end up becoming emotionally attached to their old religion and/or approach to religion. They want to stop the clock and make sure nothing changes in their religious doctrine, their culture, their church or their religious practices. This unwillingness to ride the winds of change is one of the major causes of religious conflict.

Let me give you a brief overview of spiritual cycles, starting with the lowest level, as represented by the stage of the caveman. Primitive humans were in a state of consciousness in which they had little understanding of themselves or the world around them. They were passively reacting to changes in their environment without understanding what caused such changes. They had no way to see a connection between themselves, between their own state of consciousness, and their outer situation.

After the caveman stage, people moved into a stage that was dominated by what one might call a magical consciousness. At this stage, people had begun to understand that there were certain invisible forces working in their environment. Because people had no way to explain or understand what they observed, they saw natural phenomena as the result of some kind of magical force. People had no way to clearly understand this force and thought it was random and inexplicable.

After the magical state of consciousness, people progressed in their ability to think in abstract terms. They realized that the forces behind natural phenomena were not random. There seemed to be some kind of intelligence or purpose behind the workings of nature. During this stage, people began to see this intelligence in the form of nonmaterial beings. People began to develop the concept of God.

People then started believing that the forces in their environment were the results of the actions of one or numerous gods. At this stage people still had no clear understanding of the connection between God and human beings. They did not understand that their own actions had an impact upon their outer situation. During the next phase, people developed the concept of a God who interacts with human beings. Instead of being the passive victims of the actions of the gods, people now began to understand that there is a connection between their own actions and the actions of God.

Because people were still in a relatively low state of consciousness, they developed the concept of an angry and punishing God. However, contrary to previous ages, the anger and punishment of God was not random and unintelligible. The major progress that happened during this period was that people began to understand that God's actions are determined by certain laws. God only punishes people when they violate its laws. If you understand and follow certain laws, you will improve your situation. If you violate or ignore those laws, your situation will get worse.

When I walked the earth, I brought a new concept of God. Instead of portraying God as an angry and judgmental God, I portrayed God as a loving father figure. The purpose was to help people see a more direct connection between themselves and God so they could develop a personal relationship with God. My mission was to preach and demonstrate that all people have the potential to develop a new sense of identity. By developing this new sense of identity, people can attain a correct understanding of their relationship with God, namely that all people are sons and daughters of God.

Developing a sense of identity as a son or daughter of God is not the end of spiritual growth. There is a higher stage, and during the next 2,000 years humankind must begin to fully understand that higher stage. Planet earth is moving into a new spiritual cycle, and the ascended masters are releasing certain energies that will help produce a revolutionary leap in the spiritual evolution of humankind. People must now come to the realization that they are not meant to passively follow God's laws. Instead, they are meant to internalize those creative principles so they can become co-creators with God.

That is a revolutionary concept, especially when you compare it to so many religious doctrines that portray people as being victims of God's punishment. How can people best take advantage of this opportunity?

To fully embrace the spiritual changes that are occurring, spiritually interested people must develop an understanding of what is happening. If you consider the explanation given above, you will see that people have gradually been brought to a deeper and clearer understanding of their relationship to God. Humankind has been lifted from a very primitive state of consciousness, in which they had no clear understanding of the concept of God, into a state of consciousness in which they are ready to understand, accept and embrace a correct relationship to God.

To give you an overview of the evolutionary process of religion, let us talk about the two previous ages and the coming age. During the cycle that was dominated by the Law of Moses, people were meant to come to an understanding of the laws of God. The main role of religion was to give people an understanding of these laws. Every age has a positive and a negative potential. The positive potential was that by getting to know the laws of God, people would develop the intuitive understanding that it was in their own best interest, it was enlightened self-interest, to follow these laws. They would also realize that God is not an angry God who is ready to punish the slightest transgression. God has simply created an impersonal law that you will reap as you have sown. If you sow good deeds, you reap beneficial consequences. If you violate God's law, you reap unpleasant consequences. God has no feelings involved in this. The law of cause and effect is as impersonal as the law of gravity.

The negative potential was that religion would set itself up as being the source of God's laws and the police force that was supposed to enforce those laws. Religion would become the law and religious authorities would police the people by instilling fear of God and God's punishment. Religion would then promote fear of God instead of the love-based view that God's laws are created to help people avoid destroying themselves and the planet. During the past 2,000 years, what is often called the Age of Pisces, the purpose of religion can be illustrated in my concept of the good shepherd (John 10:11). Religion was meant to go after the lost sheep and raise them into a new understanding of their identity and their relationship to God. The positive potential was that the church would be a shepherd that gently herded the sheep to a protected pasture where they could develop their sense of identity as God's children. The negative potential was that the church would start acting as a prison guard, seeking to force the sheep into a fold defined by human beings, a fold made of dualistic doctrines and dogmas that deny people's true identity.

Unfortunately, the orthodox or mainstream Christian churches turned away from the role as shepherd and instead took on the role as prison guard. During the Age of Pisces, people were meant to develop an understanding of their relationship to God and of God's laws. People should have gained a deeper understanding of how their own actions, through the impersonal laws of God, have created their current situation.

Over thousands of years, people have been raised to a higher understanding of their relationship to God. Part of this understanding is the recognition of how God creates. We of the ascended masters have gradually been raising humankind to a clearer understanding of the fact that God has created the world by using certain principles, or laws. When people understand these principles, and use their free will to align themselves with the laws of God, they can stop the self-destructive spirals that have been reinforced over thousands of years.

However, the true goal is not to simply raise people to a state of consciousness in which they stop destroying themselves. The true goal is to raise humankind to a state of consciousness in which people see themselves as co-creators with God. People must come to an understanding of the principles that God uses to create the world. They must realize that they too have the potential to use these principles and thereby help create the kingdom of God. Only by acting as co-creators with God can people become the instruments for bringing God's Kingdom to earth. That is why the Bible says:

> And God said, Let us make man in our image, after our likeness. (Genesis 1:26)

> And God blessed them, and God said unto them, Be fruitful, and multiply, and replenish the earth, and subdue it: and have dominion over the fish of the sea, and over the fowl of the air, and over every living thing that moveth upon the earth. (Genesis 1:28)

Human beings are meant to take dominion over the earth by internalizing the laws of God so they can use these laws to bring forth the kingdom of God. Thereby, they will naturally stop destroying the environment, their own bodies and each other in a fear-based quest for power and control. Instead, they will engage in a love-based quest to bring forth the lost paradise of their highest dreams. They dream about this lost heaven because the reality of Paradise on earth is put into their inward parts – their lifestreams – by God.

You talked about the kingdom of God 2,000 years ago, but I think most people see it as being up there in heaven and not down here on earth. They also think we have no chance of helping to manifest it. Are you saying that you want to bring it to earth and that you want us to help you do so?

The true goal of the ascended masters has always been to bring the kingdom of God, which truly is a state of consciousness, into the material universe. Until now, humankind has not been

5 | Why so Many Different Religions?

at a level of consciousness that made it possible to bring God's kingdom to earth. We want the inhabitants of earth to see this world as being one pocket in God's creation. We desire people to understand that my Father's house has many mansions (John 14:2) and that this universe, including planet earth, is one mansion in the House of God. One might say that in previous ages people did not see any connection between their own actions and their outer situations. They thought they were victims of forces beyond their control. People have gradually been raised to the higher understanding that the world is guided by certain laws and that a violation of those laws leads to undesirable consequences.

People now need to take another leap and realize that human beings have always been co-creators with God. People create through the power of their attention, their consciousness. People must realize that the current limitations on planet earth were not created by God but by human beings. People created limitations and suffering because they fell into the consciousness of duality. The only way to improve conditions on this planet is that people decide to create God's perfection instead of human imperfection. In order to do that, they must rise above duality by putting on the mind of Christ.

If people do flow with these spiritual cycles, does that mean a particular religion will become obsolete? Did Judaism become obsolete with your coming to earth?

That depends on whether a religion can adapt to the changes built into the spiritual cycles. I did come to inaugurate the Age of Pisces, but as I said, I did not come to start a new dogmatic religion. I came to teach and demonstrate a set of universal principles that could be incorporated into almost any existing religion. Judaism didn't automatically become obsolete because of my mission. It was the hope of the ascended masters that Judaism would be renewed, and this could have happened even without recognizing me as the Messiah.

The renewal could not happen by completely ignoring the change in consciousness that was part of the Age of Pisces—Jews had to recognize their potential to put on a higher state of consciousness. Judaism has since been renewed through the teachings of Kabbalah and thus it is not an obsolete religion. All of the old religions must be renewed again as we move into the next spiritual cycle.

The next 2,000 years, often called the Age of Aquarius, is an age of spiritual freedom in which people are meant to attain a direct, inner connection to a higher part of their own beings. We might call it the Christ self or the higher self. This is what was prophesied in the following quote:

> But they shall sit every man under his vine and under his fig tree; and none shall make them afraid: for the mouth of the LORD of hosts hath spoken it. (Micah 4:4)

The "vine and fig tree" is a symbol for your spiritual self. When you have direct contact with that self, you no longer fear any force in this world. Your approach to religion is entirely based on love. The simple fact is that in order to meet the spiritual needs of people in the Aquarian Age, a religion must transcend all exclusivism and stop presenting itself as the only true religion. The leaders of every religion must realize that, in the new age, the true purpose of religion is to help people discover the kingdom of God within them and establish a connection with that kingdom, a connection that is independent of any outer religion. A religion that insists on portraying itself as the only road to salvation, claiming the road to salvation goes through the outer religion, simply will not be able to meet the spiritual needs of its followers in this age. That is why you already see some traditional religions that are losing members at an ever-increasing rate. That is why you see so many people who are giving up on all organized or formal religion.

We are entering an age in which human beings are meant to reach the point of spiritual self-sufficiency where they will not let anything – including an outer religion or their own dualistic consciousness – stand between them and a direct experience of God's truth. A religion that understands this and seeks to support people's inner connection will still be highly relevant and will attract many followers. A religion that holds on to the old dogmatic approach can still survive, but it will attract only the type of people who refuse to change with the times.

The concept of spiritual cycles is very interesting to me because ever since childhood I sensed that there was a need for a spiritual renewal and reawakening. I have met many other people who feel the same way. What is your take on that?

Many of the open-minded people in today's world are subconsciously attuned to the spiritual energies of the time. They have the potential to become a major force that will bring a spiritual reawakening. Such an awakening is the only way to put an end to religious conflict. This is not a mere fantasy but a very real possibility. It will require that the more spiritual people recognize the need for a new approach to religion. It will require them to leave behind the old belief that there is only one true religion or that one religion will save the world.

6 | OVERCOMING THE FEAR OF CHANGE

I foresee that many people will be apprehensive about the need for change so I would like to return to your parable about the native tribe that had its religious world view collapse. I think it illustrates what has happened to a lot of people in our scientific and materialistic age. Many people have already lost their faith in all religion. Many others are scared of acknowledging the need for growth because they are afraid of losing their faith. Out of fear, they hold on to their religious doctrines as if it was a matter of life and death. How would you respond to that?

I am fully aware of the dilemma faced by many people in this age. I have no desire to see people lose their faith, yet I also see that many people are stuck in a limited approach to religion. We might call it the outer approach or the fear-based approach. It is outer because people think that following an outer religion is the only road to salvation. It is fear-based because people are afraid that if they question or look beyond the doctrines of the outer religion, they will go to hell.

This outer approach not only causes religious conflicts around the world, but it also causes individuals to suffer needlessly from fear and unresolved questions—which can jeopardize their salvation. As a spiritual teacher, it is my assignment to awaken people to the reality about salvation, as I attempted to do 2,000 years ago. You will see that back then I consistently challenged those who took the outer approach to religion. I did not come to destroy or take away people's faith in God. I came to help them replace their limited beliefs with a higher understanding.

I understand that many people were brought up to accept the outer approach to religion, and many of them feel they can no longer hold on to it. What do you lose by letting go of the fear-based approach to religion? You lose a false image of religion that springs from a dualistic view of life, and you have the opportunity to overcome your fear. I know this can be a painful process, but only if you seek to hold on to your childhood approach to religion. Instead, consider taking the next step and finding a better approach to religion. Consider basing your faith on intuitive insights instead of dualistic doctrines. This is what I always wanted and what I still want for spiritual people.

People would make things so much easier for themselves if they would accept the idea that their current understanding of religious topics might not be the highest possible. By reaching for a higher understanding, they can replace their limited beliefs without ever losing their faith in God. I am not asking people to throw away their faith and plunge themselves into a vacuum of doubting everything. I am asking them to gradually expand their understanding of God's truth, which can only strengthen their faith in God.

It is a simple fact that the world is changing. I realize that many Christians, and many other religious people, are seeking to ignore what they see as scientific attacks on religion. History proves that you cannot ignore change. Those who attempt to do so become extinct, like the dinosaurs. The dinosaurs became extinct because they could not adapt to changing circumstances. History has several examples of religions that refused to adapt and therefore became extinct.

The most constructive way to deal with the changing times is to admit that your current religious beliefs might not be the highest possible understanding of God. Once you do that, you open the door so that God can give you a higher understanding that will strengthen your faith and empower you to deal with all challenges to your faith—even those posed by scientific discoveries. On the other hand, if you hold on to your religious doctrines, insisting that they must be infallible, you set yourself up for a fall. This is what happened to the medieval Christians who held on to the so-called infallible church doctrine that the earth was the center of the universe.

Yes, but the problem is that many religious people were brought up to never question their religious doctrines. It isn't that easy for such people to let go of the idea that their religious doctrine is an absolute and infallible truth. How would you help them overcome that?

One might begin by asking them how Christianity ever got started? How did I ever attract any followers? Many Jews had been brought up with the outer approach to religion, believing the Jewish religion was the only road to salvation. As the New Testament clearly demonstrates, many of my actions and statements were offending to orthodox Jews. The reason was that my teachings went far beyond the orthodox doctrines that people believed were absolute and infallible. If everyone at the time had taken the orthodox approach to religion, I would never have attracted any followers. If everyone had closed their minds to any ideas beyond orthodox doctrines, they would have been afraid to listen to my new ideas. Consequently, I would have been walking around preaching to the birds and Christianity would have died in infancy.

Christianity proves that, in its own time, God gives people a new religious teaching. Only those who have open minds – only those who have ears to hear – will discover this new teaching. People with closed minds will be stuck in their old beliefs, waiting for whatever salvation they envision without recognizing that it has already been delivered.

Many Christians will say that there will be no new revelation because you gave us the ultimate truth and the ultimate key to salvation.

Sure they will. The reason is that they are taking the exact same outer, fear-based, closed-minded approach to religion that the orthodox people of my time used to justify their rejection of me. Most Christians believe that if they had been alive 2,000 years ago, they would have instantly recognized me as the living Christ. The unpopular truth is that most modern-day Christians would not recognize me if they bumped into me on the street.

Here is the bottom line. If you are not open to the possibility that God or myself could give teachings today that go beyond what was given in the Bible, then you would not have been open to my teachings if you had met me 2,000 years ago. You would have used orthodox doctrines to reject my "dangerous" ideas. Sadly, many of today's Christians are now using the teachings I gave 2,000 years ago to reject the possibility that I might have new teachings to give to people in this age.

Many of them even use the Bible as proof that there will be no divine revelation after you!

A very unfortunate line of reasoning that even ignores one of my own statements:

> I have yet many things to say unto you, but ye cannot bear them now. (John 16:12)

If you take an unbiased look at the Bible, you will see a clear progression. The Old Testament was based on the Law of Moses. If that had been all God wanted to say to people, the Old Testament would have ended with Exodus. Instead, God sent a string of prophets to give people new teachings and warnings. Most people overlook the fact that the prophets were not members of the orthodox religious hierarchy. They were outsiders who were often persecuted by the orthodox hierarchy and even by the people. The reason was that the prophets were sent to challenge orthodox doctrines and interpretations. This was done because orthodoxy had moved away from the true purpose of religion and had become stuck in the outer, fear-based approach. The orthodox leaders had lost the key of knowledge and were not open to any new revelation from above. God had to choose a prophet from outside the orthodox hierarchy, a person who was open to God's Living Word. As I have said before, the dualistic mind creates mental images and projects them upon reality. People have used the dualistic mind to create mental images of God, and it makes some people believe that God thinks the way they do and would agree with their interpretation of scripture. They cannot even imagine that God is not trapped in their mental box. In reality, God is fully aware of how the dualistic state of mind causes people to impose relative interpretations upon any spiritual teaching. God realizes that it is just a matter of time before a religion becomes stuck in orthodoxy and replaces a genuine search for the Spirit of Truth with blind adherence to outer doctrines. When this happens, God attempts to send people a prophet or messenger who can renew the outer religion. If the hierarchy and a majority of the followers of the old religion refuse to heed God's messenger, then God might abandon the old religion and create a new one. That is exactly what happened with Christianity. Because I was rejected by the Jewish religious establishment, Judaism was not renewed and a new religion emerged. This does not necessarily mean that a religion is abandoned forever, and, as already mentioned, Judaism was renewed through the teachings of Kabbalah.

It is extremely dangerous and prideful to assume that any religion is above the mechanism that causes people to become stuck in the outer approach to religion. Pride makes you blind, and it was pride that prevented so many people from accepting my new teachings. Today, many Christians are likewise blinded by pride and that is why they are not open to anything beyond the doctrines they have defined as the only truth, the only true church and the only road to salvation.

Some say there is no need for revelation beyond what you gave us, and they use this statement as their "infallible" proof:

> Think not that I am come to destroy the law, or the prophets: I am not come to destroy, but to fulfill. (Matthew 5:17)

6 | Overcoming the Fear of Change

They say that because you fulfilled the law and the prophets, there is no need for any further revelation.

That is a good example of how the dualistic state of mind can cause people to develop mental images that prevent them from experiencing truth. I just quoted the statement that I had yet many things to say to people but that they could not bear them at the time. The truth behind that statement is that I never intended to leave people with no further revelation. It also shows that when I walked the earth, humankind was in a state of consciousness that prevented me from giving them the full truth about God. This is also proven by the following quote:

> But without a parable spake he not unto them: and when they were alone, he expounded all things to his disciples. (Mark 4:34)

I could not tell the multitudes everything, and that is why I spoke in parables. This was not due to a limitation on my part but a limitation in people's level of consciousness. My disciples were in a somewhat higher state of consciousness than the multitudes – which is why they were willing to leave everything behind to follow me – so I could give them a higher teaching.

Remember what I said earlier, namely that the purpose of religion is to lead people to a higher state of consciousness. The conclusion is that when God gives people a religious teaching, the teaching is not meant to give people an absolute truth that will be complete for all time. The teaching is carefully adapted to the level of consciousness of the target audience. It is meant to lead them from their present level of consciousness to a higher level. When people apply the teaching given, they will rise to a higher level of consciousness, and then God can give them a more advanced teaching. My intent was that, as people applied my new teachings, they would grow in awareness, which would allow me to release more advanced teachings. For example, when the multitudes had applied my public teachings, I would be able to give them the teachings I gave to my disciples.

That leads me to fundamentalism. It sounds to me like fundamentalists are basically saying that they don't want to go beyond a certain level and receive a higher understanding of truth?

They are saying that they don't want to go beyond their present level of understanding, which is likely to be the level of understanding that people had when their religious teaching was released from above. That teaching might not necessarily be kindergarten level. Even a very advanced spiritual teaching can become a trap if people think it is absolute and infallible and refuse to look beyond it. This is a subtle point overlooked by most religious people. It is quite possible to take a true spiritual teaching, given by the ascended masters, and turn it into a false teaching by creating the belief system that the teaching is an infallible truth and there is nothing beyond it. Thereby, the true teaching, given to set your mind free from duality, becomes overlaid with a false teaching that traps you even more firmly in duality. Unfortunately, this is the story of most religions on this planet. It is true that today's fundamentalist Christians are refusing to go beyond the level of consciousness that many people had 2,000 years ago. Such people are not understanding the true purpose of religion, but think a scripture is meant to be absolute and infallible, meaning that it could never change.

I have had some discussions with fundamentalist Christians, and I have a hard time understanding their mindset. It seems like there is no way to truly reach them and make them even consider anything beyond what they have decided is the only true interpretation of the Bible.

Welcome to the club! Now you know how I felt when I stood before the fundamentalist Jews who accused me of blasphemy because I said something that was beyond their literal interpretations of the scriptures.

You mean that fundamentalism is not limited to Christianity?

Of course not. You can find fundamentalists in every religion, even in the field of science. The people engaged in Jihad are obviously fundamentalist Muslims. Fundamentalism is a universal mindset that springs from a mechanism in the human psyche. I know some anti-religious people claim that it is a particular religion that encourages fundamentalism. In reality, it is the outer approach – the fear-based approach – to religion that encourages fundamentalism and not the original spiritual teaching.

You mean the fundamentalist mindset springs from the consciousness of duality and that it causes people to believe the ends can justify the means?

Exactly. Otherwise how could the fundamentalist Jews have justified killing the person who had been appointed by God to bring forth a new spiritual teaching as a gift to humankind? It was precisely the fundamentalist mindset that caused these people to feel threatened by the fact that some of my actions and statements contradicted their literal interpretations. They were so threatened by this that they were willing to do anything to silence me. They wanted to remove my new teachings that were urging them to change, and the reason was that they were completely unwilling to change, unwilling to grow. They had put God in a mental box, and they felt so comfortable in that box that they didn't want God's messenger to challenge their sense of security.

Why did they feel so threatened by your statements—I mean why do people feel threatened by truth? Don't all people want truth?

As a matter of fact, many people do not want truth and this is a major problem for the spiritual teachers of humankind. The ugly fact is that many people live in an illusion, but they are comfortable in that illusion. They don't want someone to disturb them with the truth. The fundamentalist mindset – and the outer approach to religion – is based on a rather complex psychological mechanism, and it will take some time to explain it. Would you like me to do so?

Yes, I really would like to understand this because I don't see how we can overcome religious conflict as long as people are caught in the fundamentalist mindset.

I earlier said that the story of the Garden of Eden was meant to illustrate what has happened to every lifestream. I realize that any fundamentalist will immediately reject this idea, but then again, it is not likely that a fundamentalist will read this book. Let us consider that the Garden of Eden might have been a spiritual schoolroom for lifestreams. In the Garden, all lifestreams had direct contact with a spiritual teacher, who was teaching them how to exercise their creativity within the safe framework of God's laws. The Bible calls the teacher "God" because people were not ready for a more detailed understanding and considered any spiritual being as God.

In order to exercise creativity, you have to be able to make choices. A sculptor sitting with a lump of clay has the potential to model numerous figures with that clay, yet only one can actually be modeled. The sculptor has to choose which one of the many possibilities will be made manifest. God gave every lifestream free will, and, as mentioned earlier, it is an inevitable consequence of free will that the lifestream can choose to go against God's law.

The Garden of Eden was set up to educate lifestreams in the art of exercising their creativity without harming themselves or the whole of which they are a part. As I said, you can do this only when you know God's law and see yourself as part of the whole. The fruit of the knowledge of good and evil is a state of consciousness. The essence of it is that the lifestream no longer defines its actions based on the rock of God's law – the rock of Christ – but on the shifting sands of its own mental images (Matthew 7:24-27). The lifestream replaces truth with its own relative definition of good and evil—and then it firmly beliefs this is the absolute truth.

One might say that, in the eyes of God, there is no good and evil, meaning that there is no value judgment. Something is either one with God's law or apart from it, and that is an absolute standard which implies no value judgment—it either is or it isn't and there is nothing in between. When a lifestream slips into duality, it begins to think in terms of good and bad, which are graded values that can be put on a scale with many values in between two extremes. Something can be partially good or bad, and now we have the possibility of a value judgment. The lifestream can define a new standard that forms an idol, a graven image, to obscure the absolute standard of God. When people use such a relative standard, it is quite possible that they can define an act as good, yet that act is still a violation of God's law. People can be doing what they define as good, while in reality their beliefs and actions are bringing them no closer to union with God. One example is that people can kill in the name of God. I exposed this human tendency to create a false standard, a false sense of righteousness, in the following quote:

> For I say unto you, That except your righteousness shall exceed the righteousness of the scribes and Pharisees, ye shall in no case enter into the kingdom of heaven. (Matthew 5:20)

When the lifestream partakes of the dualistic state of consciousness, it will begin to see itself as separated from its source and from the whole. The lifestream now sees itself as being *apart from* God instead of being *a part of* God. The person also sees itself as being separated from other people, and this is where the potential for conflict enters the consciousness of the soul. As long as you see yourself as one with all life, you will know that if you harm another person, you are harming yourself. No conflict exists. As soon as you see yourself as being separated from others, it is possible to believe in the illusion that you can harm someone else without harming yourself. You think you can harm others without reaping what you have sown. In reality, all life is interconnected, as both the Bible and modern science states, but it is possible for the soul to create the mental illusion that life is separated by barriers. These barriers exist only in the mind, but as long as the lifestream maintains the illusion, it will act based on the illusion. This is what causes all human conflict.

Tell me how both the Bible and science show that all life is interconnected.

The Gospel of John starts with these words:

> 1 In the beginning was the Word, and the Word was with God, and the Word was God.
> 2 The same was in the beginning with God.
> 3 All things were made by him; and without him was not any thing made that was made.

If you are trapped by duality, you cannot understand this passage, but when you begin to see beyond duality, you see the hidden meaning. What is said here is that the universe was created by God—who created any thing that was made. A "thing" can be defined as something that has form. God is the source of all form. However, because all things were created by God, it follows that God was beyond form. God existed before there was any form, which means that God is not confined to any form. God is formless, which is why several religions talk about the "void" or say that God is unknowable. This is the real meaning behind the first two commandments that we mentioned earlier. Because God is beyond form, you cannot create any form and claim that the form captures the totality of God. If you do so, you have created a graven image and you are worshipping an idol, a false God. We can also say that God is unknowable in the sense that no description in words can capture the fullness of God but your mind has the capacity to directly experience God's Presence. That is why you have to "worship" God in spirit and in truth.

If God is the creator of all form and is beyond form, it follows that "in the beginning," meaning before any form had been created, there was only God. Nothing but God existed.

I am not sure I understand that.

Everything in the created world has form so God has no form. Forms are defined by certain characteristics that set them apart from each other. A circle is different from a square. If God is beyond form, it follows that there are no differentiations or separations in God. God is an undivided whole. If there are no divisions in God, there cannot be anything that is separate from or different from God so God must be all there is.

The logical consequence is that if God is all there is, it follows that even though God is almighty, it has one limitation. Given that God is all there is, God cannot create anything that is different from or apart from itself. God has to create everything out of itself, and that is why the Bible says: "Without him was not any thing made that was made." God created all form out of its own being, its own consciousness. God started by envisioning the form it wanted to create, and in order to give that form its characteristics, God used the Word. God defined the form by describing it through the Word. But even the Word "was God" as the Bible clearly states.

Most Christians – and many other religious people – do believe we live in a world that is separated from God. They think that is why we need to be saved.

Of course they do, but that belief springs from the consciousness of duality, the consciousness of separation. People who are trapped in this state of mind cannot see beyond the created forms. Some of them are so trapped in duality that they believe there is nothing beyond the material universe. They think that only what they can detect with their senses or scientific instruments has any reality, and that is why they often deny the existence of God.

Others are not as trapped in duality, and they can accept the idea that there is something beyond the visible world, namely the spiritual world and God. Their image of this hidden world is very much influenced by the consciousness of duality, and that is why they see themselves as separated from God. They think God is far above them, and they cannot accept the fact that "every thing that was made" was created out of God's Being.

If everything is created by God, does that mean God created suffering or evil?

No, and here is why. The Bible states:

> And God said, Let us make man in our image, after our likeness: and let them have dominion... (Genesis 1:26)

The truth is that the lifestream was originally created after God's image and likeness, meaning that the lifestream is a self-conscious being with the ability to create by using the laws and the light of God. After the lifestream fell into the consciousness of duality, it no longer created after God's image and likeness, meaning God's law. Instead, human beings started creating based on their own dualistic images of what they considered to be reality.

Because God gave lifestreams dominion over the earth, God will not interfere. God will literally let humankind destroy the earth rather than violate their free will. Obviously, this does not mean that God has abandoned humankind or that God wants people to destroy themselves. If people ask for God's intercession, they will receive it. If nobody asks, God will let people create their own private hell on earth. God created a universe that acts as a mirror. As you sow, so shall you reap (Galatians 6:7). When you create something that is out of alignment with God's laws, it is not sustainable. Your creation will inevitably begin to break down and this is what leads to suffering. The suffering presently seen on earth is simply a temporary phenomenon that humankind has collectively created based on the consciousness of duality.

That makes a lot of sense. I have always wondered how people could possibly do some of the more atrocious things they do. How could a human being have precipitated the Holocaust and other mind-numbing atrocities? You seem to be saying that this all springs from the sense of separation from the whole so we think we can kill others without harming ourselves in the process?

Yes, but it probably helps when you realize that when God gave lifestreams free will, it knew that they could potentially misuse it to separate themselves from the whole. In so doing they could harm the whole, including themselves. Free will does not exist alone; it is paired with the law of cause and effect, which ensures that you will reap what you have sown. Whatever you create, you will inevitably experience. If you sow the wind, you will reap the whirlwind (Hosea 8:7). As I said, the universe is a mirror that reflects back to you whatever you send out. Whatever you do unto others, the universe will do to you because you are doing it to the whole. Because you are part of that whole, you are doing it to yourself:

> And the King shall answer and say unto them, Verily I say unto you, Inasmuch as ye have done it unto one of the least of these my brethren, ye have done it unto me. (Matthew 25:40)

Now, before we get too far afield, let me get back to your question of how religion and science show unity. We have now seen that the Bible clearly demonstrates that "every thing that was made" was made from God's substance and has God's Presence within it.

Many Christians will say that this idea in Pantheism and that it is a Pagan idea.

Sure, and then those same Christians turn around and celebrate Christmas on December 25th, which is – as a matter of indisputable historical fact – a Pagan holiday absorbed by Christianity. When people are trapped in duality, they love to create little labels and use them to judge ideas beyond their accepted belief system. Fear-based Christians have given every idea that is beyond their literal interpretation a label, and they have decided that such ideas are automatically bad or of the devil.

Unfortunately, these people don't understand the inner meaning of my call to do unto others as you want them to do unto you. The deeper meaning is that – because the universe is a mirror – what you do unto others, you do unto yourself. By labeling and judging other people, you are confining yourself to a mental box that is limited by your judgment of others. You become trapped by your own judgments, which is precisely what happened to the people who killed me. As I said:

> For with what judgment ye judge, ye shall be judged: and with what measure ye mete, it shall be measured to you again. (Matthew 7:2)

People who are trapped in the consciousness of duality will never be able to accept that God is in everything. Their state of consciousness is based on separation, which is a denial of the basic fact that all life is interconnected because it came from the same source. In reality, as I have now tried to explain from several perspectives, this denial is a violation of the first two commandments.

Some people have created a mental image of a God who is separated from themselves, and they worship this idol instead of the true God who is in every thing that was made. The simple fact is that if you do not accept that God is where you are – if you do not accept that the kingdom of God is within you – then you are denying God where you are. This denial of God is blasphemy—and there are no two ways about it. You either accept that God is everywhere or you deny God's presence where you are. You either choose life or you choose death.

You will note that whenever I even hinted that I had overcome duality and developed a sense of oneness with God, the fundamentalist Jews accused me of blasphemy. It is the fundamentalists – Jews, Christians or any other denomination – who are guilty of blasphemy, and they are committing blasphemy with every thought, feeling, word and act that affirms the concept of separation. No man-made label or mental box can contain or confine the reality of God and the truth of Christ. The human ego loves to judge other people. The inner meaning of my statement: "Judge not, that ye be not judged" (Matthew

7:1) is that if you create a mental box and judge others, you will end up being trapped by your own dualistic judgments.

How has science shown the unity of all things?

During the 1900s, in what is called "classical physics," it was believed that all matter particles were separate entities. If two particles were separated by space, they could affect each other only when a signal was sent from one particle to the other. It was also believed that no signal could be sent faster than the speed of light.

In the last few decades this view has been challenged by both theory and experiment. It has been shown that two matter particles can be separated in space, yet a change in one particle can instantly be reflected as a change in the characteristics of the other particle. This instant communication implies that there is a deeper reality beyond the reality of the senses or time/space. We might say that even though the two particles are separated in space, they are actually not separated from each other. They are connected at the level of a deeper reality, and that is why a change in one particle can be instantly reflected in the other. There is no need to send a signal between them because they are both part of a larger whole. Einstein even had a name for this whole; he called it the "space-time continuum."

It is an indisputable fact that science is currently in a transition phase. Most scientists realize they have discovered the limitations of current paradigms without having found a suitable replacement. I predict that a new world view will be found when scientists overcome the dualistic, fundamentalist mindset that causes them to cling to materialism.

Anyway, to make a long story short, both science and religion indicate that all life is interconnected because it is part of a larger whole. The problem is, of course, that some parts of that whole are not visible to the human senses and cannot be understood by people who are trapped in the consciousness of duality and separation. That is why some people deny the inter-connectedness of all created things. Even though we have taken a long detour, we have actually gained some insights we can use to explain what happened to the lifestream as it began to experiment with the fruit of the knowledge of good and evil.

The last thing I said was that the lifestream creates the illusion that some parts of the whole are separated by barriers, for example that it is separated from other people and can harm them without harming itself. Contrary to the Bible's concept of one defining event, the creation of this illusion was a gradual process. The lifestream very gradually started creating the illusion of separation, and this happened so slowly that the lifestream did not realize that it was getting caught in its own trap.

However, at one point the lifestream had a moment of truth, and it realized that it had separated itself from God, or rather from its spiritual teacher. The lifestream did not realize that this sense of separation was an illusion because it had created the illusion so gradually that it had come to believe it was real. At the moment of truth, the lifestream suddenly came to the awareness that it was separated from God and that it could not hide this from God. The lifestream felt "naked" in that it could not hide its state of consciousness from the teacher.

Here comes an all-important point that is not explained in the Bible. There were actually some lifestreams in the Garden of Eden who went back to the teacher, confessed their "sin" of having partaken of the duality consciousness and asked for forgiveness. These lifestreams received the loving guidance of the teacher on how to rise above their self-created illusion by putting on the mind of Christ.

Unfortunately, some lifestreams decided that they were not willing to go back and stand naked before the teacher. In order to prevent the teacher from seeing their "nakedness," they turned away from the teacher and attempted to hide. One might say that since lifestreams fell into the dualistic consciousness, the ascended masters have attempted to offer them a systematic path to Christhood. We have given this path in many disguises, depending on the time and culture in which it appeared. In every case, it was our hope that we could lead lifestreams back to Eden so they could re-establish a direct contact with their spiritual teachers.

The lifestream has free will and the teacher of the lifestream will not violate that free will. If the lifestream turns away from the teacher, the teacher cannot help that person overcome the illusion. The teacher must let the lifestream venture into the world created by its own illusion of separation. This is what the Bible portrays in the rather ominous description of how Adam and Eve were cast out of the Garden by angels with flaming swords (Genesis 3:24). The reality is that the lifestream casts itself out by enveloping itself in the illusions of separation, until it can no longer perceive the spiritual realm. The lifestream is then trapped in the "outer darkness" created by its own dualistic illusions (Matthew 22:13).

My point for taking you through this long discourse is to show you the psychological mechanism that causes lifestreams to turn away from the teacher. The underlying mechanism is always fear. As long as the lifestream has a sense of oneness with its source, it has no fear of God. How could it fear something of which it is a part and which it sees as a loving Being? The moment the lifestream begins to think it is separated from God, at that moment fear inevitably enters its consciousness. The basic fear is that the lifestream could be lost, meaning that it could be permanently separated from God, that the lifestream could die in a spiritual sense. This fear is an illusion because, as I said, no part of God could ever be apart from God. Because of the consciousness of duality, the lifestream cannot see that the fear is an illusion. It can become consumed by the fear, and because this fear is unbearable, the lifestream has to find a way to alleviate the fear so that it can live with it.

Of course, the lifestream could alleviate the fear by going back to the teacher, but the fear prevents it from doing that so the lifestream is in a catch-22. There are two basic reactions that can prevent the lifestream from going back:

- Some lifestreams not only create the illusion of separation, but they use the consciousness of duality to create a false image of God as being angry and judgmental. They now become afraid of going back to the teacher because they think they will be punished. In an attempt to avoid this imagined punishment, they run away from the teacher. Their fear of loss prevents them from doing the one thing that could save them from what they fear.

- Some lifestreams develop the image that God is unreasonable and has treated them unfairly or that he should never have given them free will. They are not consumed by fear but deflect it into one of the more subtle manifestations of fear, namely pride. Pride is also based on the consciousness of separation in that the lifestream believes it is somehow better than others. When you realize all lifestreams come from the same source, you see that they all have the same value in the eyes of God. Or rather, God does not make relative judgments so comparison has no meaning.

The prideful lifestreams now reason that they do not want to go back to the teacher or that they can make it without the teacher. Basically, they think they either have not made a mistake or that they can make it back to God without admitting their mistake. They turn their backs on the teacher, thinking they can somehow find a way to be saved without the teacher.

How do these reactions manifest in the fundamentalist mindset? The problem we have is that the lifestream is trapped by fear. Fear always springs from illusion and it is a fear of loss, which makes it unbearable. The person simply cannot live with the fear. Because the person is unwilling to examine the illusion – the consciousness of duality – that created the fear, it cannot permanently remove the fear. If you dare not look at the illusion that created your fears, you cannot free yourself from those fears. When a person cannot overcome its fear, it must seek to deflect it, and it attempts to do so by creating a new illusion that enables it to control the fear.

In creating this illusion, the lifestream can take any number of roads because there is almost no limit to the beliefs that can be created from the consciousness of duality. Once the lifestream has lost contact with God's truth, it can continue building layer upon layer of illusion, each layer taking the lifestream further and further away, not from truth but from a clear experience of truth. The lifestream is creating a mental box based entirely on illusion, and this box becomes its prison.

Some people create a mental box that denies the existence of God, enabling them to explain away the fear as being irrational. Some people have not descended that far into illusion, and they cannot ignore or deny God. Instead they create an image of God that enables them to control their fear. One such image is the idea that God is an angry God, but that he can be appeased through an outer sacrifice. Throughout the ages, many cultures have believed in sacrifice, even human sacrifice. Unfortunately, many Christians believe in the idea that my crucifixion was the ultimate human sacrifice that appeased the angry God and set them free from all their sins. Other Christians think that as long as they believe in an outer doctrine and follow a set of rigid rules, they will some day be saved by an outer savior. Their motivation for following the rules is to avoid punishment and to qualify for an automatic salvation. They are seeking to buy their way into heaven.

Still others are trapped in pride, and they actually believe they know better than God what is required for salvation. They believe that their religion, and their interpretation of its scriptures, is the only right one. They belong to an elite whose members are guaranteed to be saved. They think they can be saved through outer measures without changing their consciousness, without confronting their fears or abandoning their pride. This is the illusion held by the scribes and Pharisees.

The conclusion to all this is that once lifestreams have become trapped by their self-created illusions, they feel a certain sense of false security, a security based on control. They feel they have their fears under control, and thus they can live with them, even though they have not been resolved. This explains why many people are completely unwilling to consider any idea that goes beyond their chosen beliefs. If their illusion was threatened, their sense of control would slip away, and they would be thrown back into an unbearable fear. Or they might be forced to admit that their pride was based on an illusion.

The more a person is trapped in fear, the more reluctant it will be to let go of its sense of control, and it will be highly unwilling to consider any idea that goes beyond its beliefs. The person sees any new idea as a threat to its sense of security. If the person's fear or pride is very strong, it will see any threat as a life-and-death issue, and the person will be ready to do anything to maintain its sense of control. This includes killing the people who espouse ideas that threaten its illusion. After all, killing someone is the permanent way to silence the voice that threatens the illusion.

Aside from certain insane people, no normal human being will kill others. Because all life has a survival instinct, any person can become willing to kill if he or she feels that life is threatened. If you identify fully with your religious beliefs, you will think that a threat to those beliefs is a threat to your life and your way of life, possibly even a threat to the survival of the human race, the planet or the universe. You become willing to kill the people who are threatening your survival. I know this was a very long explanation, but do you see the mechanism at work?

I can see many situations in which I was either too afraid to admit I was wrong or too proud to do so. In some cases, I was not particularly nice to the people who threatened my sense of security by either questioning my beliefs or pointing out flaws in my actions. I think what you are talking about here must be a tendency that every person has. The fundamentalists might have taken it to the extreme, but all of us have this beam in our own eyes.

Yes, but once you see this tendency, admit that it keeps you trapped in a prison and decide that you are willing to overcome it, you have taken the essential step on the road that leads you back to your Father's kingdom. The problem with the fundamentalist mindset is that it prevents people from seeing that they are trapped, and they have no chance of freeing themselves. Some of them believe it is dangerous to consider any idea beyond their fundamentalist beliefs because doing so will condemn them to hell. They stay in their own self-created mental hell, all the while believing they will automatically be saved. Others are so proud that they believe they know better than anyone else, and therefore any idea beyond their interpretations is simply wrong and of the devil. I am not saying this to condemn these people. I am a spiritual teacher, and it is my assignment from God to save every lifestream on earth. I am not here to condemn any lifestream, as I said:

> For God sent not his Son into the world to condemn the world; but that the world through him might be saved. (John 3:17)

As I explained earlier, I cannot save any lifestream against its free will. I am naturally very concerned when people lock themselves in a mental box and throw away the key—the key of knowledge. Such people are literally unreachable for me because I obviously cannot violate God's Law of Free Will—not even to save a lifestream. I must simply watch as a person slides deeper and deeper into its dualistic state of consciousness, even using my own teachings to cement the belief that the lifestream is separated from God.

I am not happy about the fact that so many lifestreams are sitting in their mental prisons, feeling absolutely certain that I will some day appear in the sky to save them. At the same time, they are unwilling to let me show them the way that leads to their true salvation by raising them above the illusions of the death consciousness through the mind of Christ. These people are actually using the outer teachings of Christ to reject Christ. The rejection of Christ is anti-christ, thus these people call themselves Christians while they are following anti-christ. Take note of my statement:

> Ye are of your father the devil, and the lusts of your father ye will do. He was a murderer from the beginning, and abode not in the truth, because there is no truth in him. When he speaketh a lie, he speaketh of his own: for he is a liar, and the father of it. (John 8:44)

The devil is the father of lies because he represents the archetype of a lifestream that has become trapped by the illusion of separation. One might say that the concept of a devil is simply a way to illustrate the consciousness of separation, the consciousness of denial. I am not hereby denying the fact that some self-conscious beings identified themselves fully with that consciousness and became personal exponents of it. I am simply saying that the epic battle between good and evil is essentially a battle between two states of consciousness, namely the consciousness of Christ and the consciousness of anti-christ.

The essence of the Christ consciousness is that you see yourself as one with the whole, one with your source. When you overcome all illusion of separation, you realize the same truth that I expressed in my statement:

> I and my Father are one. (John 10:30)

This statement does not apply exclusively to me but is true for every lifestream that overcomes the illusion of separation. The consciousness of Christ is the consciousness of oneness, and the consciousness of anti-christ is the consciousness of separation—the denial of yourself as part of the whole created by God. The sad truth is that many Christians are using my teachings to lock themselves in a prison that prevents them from entering our Father's kingdom—the kingdom within them. To me, this is an amazing tragedy that I have a very strong desire to see eradicated from the earth.

I can certainly understand that desire, but I don't think it is likely to be fulfilled any time soon. I think I can foresee exactly how fundamentalists would react to what you have said. They would say that because some of your statements contradict the Bible, you cannot possibly be the real Jesus, and therefore this book is the work of the devil.

Unfortunately, you are correct and the reason is that these people are not looking for truth. It is not their goal in life to find God's truth. Their main goal is to uphold their sense of security, which means upholding their illusion. They have decided what truth is, and they are only looking for ideas that confirm what they believe is the only truth. Anything that does not confirm what they think is truth – but which is truly a dualistic illusion – is automatically rejected because it is seen as a threat to their sense of security.

Why do people need an absolute truth; what is the psychological mechanism behind it?

As I said, the lifestream that separates itself from God becomes subject to the fear that it could lose its "life," meaning its self-awareness. This is the absolute fear of every self-aware being, and that is why those who are completely lost in duality need an absolute truth in order to be able to live with the absolute fear.

How could you possibly make these people see through their illusion? I think what you are saying here makes a lot of sense, but the problem is that the people who are trapped in the mindset that leads to religious conflict are not likely to accept any of what you have said. How can these people possibly change their minds, and thus how could we possibly eradicate religious conflict?

I understand your frustration, but I don't share it. I have given you these teachings because you are open to a deeper understanding of the cause of religious conflict. It was never my intention to try to convert the people who are completely trapped in the consciousness of duality. Most of them are not convertible so it is not possible to eradicate religious conflict by trying to convert these people.

I don't understand. How in the world would it be possible to eradicate religious conflict if we can't work with the very people who cause religious wars? I thought the whole point of this discussion was to help these people see the light?

I never gave you that impression. Let me explain how we can eradicate religious conflict.

7 | WHO CAN STOP RELIGIOUS CONFLICT?

How can we stop religious conflict if we can't change the minds of the very people who actually start religious wars?

We can do so by recognizing the fact that the people who have the drive to start religious conflicts are *not* the people who have the power to stop religious conflicts. Those who actually go out to kill in the name of God – or otherwise hurt people in the name of religion – are completely blinded by duality. They have become unbalanced, and they are the blind followers of the blind leaders. Both of them will end up in the ditch of duality, separation and fanaticism (Matthew 15:14). They cannot remain on the straight and narrow – meaning balanced – path that leads to God's kingdom of oneness (Matthew 7:14).

We have seen that the cause of all conflict is the consciousness of duality, or separation. We can now create a scale that illustrates the level of people's consciousness. At the top of this scale, we have the Christ consciousness, in which you see yourself as one with God and one with all life. You see that you are part of the whole, and you are always aware that what is best for you is what is best for the whole. You are completely unselfish. As you move away from this sense of oneness – as you move deeper into the consciousness of separation and duality – you gradually lose awareness of the whole and your oneness with it. You become increasingly focused on yourself as a separate entity. To put it bluntly, you become increasingly selfish and egotistical.

At the higher stages of consciousness, you are still aware that the whole exists, and you retain some awareness of being connected to it. You can understand God's laws, such as the Law of Free Will, meaning that you respect the free will of others. As you slide deeper into separation, you become increasingly blind and self-centered and eventually you cross a threshold. You now begin to believe that the ends can justify the means, meaning that it now seems acceptable to violate God's law – such as the command not to kill – in order to further the cause that you have defined as God's cause. In reality, it is not God's cause but a self-centered cause. You are trying to control others because your sense of security is threatened by those who have different beliefs. You have lost the respect for the Law of Free Will and believe it is acceptable to violate the free will of others when it serves what you define as a "good" cause.

At the top of the scale of consciousness, you have a clear vision of the reality that all life springs from the one source, and at the bottom of the scale you have total spiritual blindness, which makes a person completely and utterly self-centered. The people who are trapped in total selfishness are beyond any illusion that they are doing God's work, and they know they are deliberately working against God's purpose—although they often hide it from others. At least they are not lying to themselves.

7 | Who Can Stop Religious Conflict?

Many of the people who are not quite as trapped in selfishness are unable and unwilling to see that what they define as a higher cause is actually a self-centered illusion. These people are the hypocrites, and some of them will feel completely justified in killing others in the name of God. The most selfish people might use religion as an excuse for getting others to kill, but they do not truly believe the killing is justified by God. They simply don't care about justifying anything because they believe that their selfish interests are their own justification.

At a slightly higher level of consciousness, you find people who are not completely selfish so they do need a justification for their actions. Because they are trapped in hypocrisy, they are easily manipulated by those who are more selfish and more calculating. Or they are deceived by their own pride and fear. If you place humankind on this scale of consciousness, you can roughly divide people into three categories:

- You have the bottom ten percent of the population, and they are the most selfish. This includes the ones who believe their desires need no justification and the worst of the hypocrites. These people will instigate religious conflict, either because it suits their selfish needs or because they truly believe it is justifiable. These people will aggressively pursue what they see as their cause—and for most of them the real cause is the attainment of power and control intertwined with the gratification of their egos.

- You have the eighty percent of the general population, and they are trapped in duality and somewhat selfish. They do not normally believe the ends can justify the means so they would never instigate religious conflict nor would they participate in it if they had a way out.

However, they can be manipulated into supporting or taking part in it. These people will not instigate a religious war, but they can be pulled into it by the lowest ten percent. Eighty percent of the population are followers, and they do not aggressively pursue any cause beyond their personal lives. They just want to live comfortable lives without being disturbed by anyone. However, if they are exposed to pressure from the outside, they will take what, at the time, seems to be the path of least resistance.

- You have the top ten percent of the population, and they are the ones who are the least selfish, meaning that they are able to, at least partially, see beyond the consciousness of duality and separation. However, their respect for other people's free will often causes them to take a passive, live and let live, approach to life. They do not want to step up to a leadership position. As a wise man once said, for evil to triumph, it only takes that good people do nothing.

Take note that when I say the top ten percent, people who are trapped in duality will immediately think that these are the recognized leaders of society, such as the political, business, intellectual or religious elite. This is just another self-centered illusion. In reality, I am talking about the people with the highest level of Christ consciousness, and they are often unrecognized for the simple reason that people trapped in duality cannot see anything valuable about these people—as they could not recognize the Living Christ when I walked the earth. The top ten percent are the people who have a sense of oneness with all life, which makes them nonviolent. They are the people about which I said:

3 Blessed are the poor in spirit: for theirs is the kingdom of heaven.

4 Blessed are they that mourn: for they shall be comforted.
5 Blessed are the meek: for they shall inherit the earth.
6 Blessed are they which do hunger and thirst after righteousness: for they shall be filled.
7 Blessed are the merciful: for they shall obtain mercy.
8 Blessed are the pure in heart: for they shall see God.
9 Blessed are the peacemakers: for they shall be called the children of God.
10 Blessed are they which are persecuted for righteousness' sake: for theirs is the kingdom of heaven.
11 Blessed are ye, when men shall revile you, and persecute you, and shall say all manner of evil against you falsely, for my sake.
12 Rejoice, and be exceeding glad: for great is your reward in heaven: for so persecuted they the prophets which were before you.
13 Ye are the salt of the earth: but if the salt have lost his savour, wherewith shall it be salted? It is thenceforth good for nothing, but to be cast out, and to be trodden under foot of men.
14 Ye are the light of the world. A city that is set on an hill cannot be hid.
15 Neither do men light a candle, and put it under a bushel, but on a candlestick; and it giveth light unto all that are in the house.
16 Let your light so shine before men, that they may see your good works, and glorify your Father which is in heaven. (Matthew, Chapter 4)

The meek shall inherit the earth because they are the ones who are aligned with the laws of God, especially the Law of Love, which has the potential to prevail over those who are trapped in duality and separation. Unless these people dare to let their light shine before men and accept their responsibility to lead the general population, positive change will not happen. The general population will either follow the bottom ten percent down into a self-destructive spiral, or they will follow the top ten percent into an upward spiral. The top ten percent of the population are the people with the potential to lift the consciousness of humankind. It is only by lifting the consciousness of humankind that we can stop religious conflict.

Exactly how does that work?

We have already talked about the fact that all life is interconnected. The reality is that everything is interconnected because it is made from the same substance, namely the consciousness of God. Everything has a certain level of consciousness, but obviously only higher life-forms have a high level of consciousness, with human beings as the only creatures on earth having self-consciousness—or at least the potential to attain self-consciousness. The higher the level of consciousness, the stronger the connection. Human beings are connected by a much stronger force than the members of an animal species. Because of free will, people can create artificial barriers that obscure this connection.

Scientists have found much evidence of such interconnections in living creatures. For example, experiments have shown that if you take a group of rats and teach a few of them to navigate a maze to find food, it becomes easier for the rest of the group to learn how to get through the maze. Likewise, it has been shown that college students today find it much easier to learn the theory of relativity than did students in the past. We might say that humankind has a collective consciousness, as pointed out by Carl Jung and other psychologists. Once a certain trail has been blazed through that consciousness, it becomes easier for others to follow. We might compare the collective consciousness of humankind to a dense jungle where it is easy to lose your way. When one person finds a way out of the jungle, he or she will carve a trail that others can follow. The more people who follow the trail, the wider it becomes, making it even easier for others to follow.

In essence, this is the process that has brought about all human progress in terms of knowledge, culture and beliefs. A few people are the trailblazers, and once a good trail has been carved, the majority of the population can follow it in stages, depending on their level of consciousness. This is the process that I described in my statement:

> And I, if I be lifted up from the earth, will draw all men unto me. (John 12:32)

In my case, I came specifically to carve a trail that can lead people to Christ consciousness. I am obviously not the only person who has served as a trailblazer for humankind. Other spiritual leaders have done so, as have many thinkers, writers, scientists, inventors and artists. Thereby, all of these people have contributed to the forward movement of humankind. In reality, every single person who expands his or her mind is contributing to the progression of humankind's consciousness.

My statement shows that if only one person raises his or her consciousness, it will create a magnetic pull on the rest of humankind. It is much like lifting one corner of a table cloth. In the beginning, you are raising only one small corner, but if you keep pulling, you will eventually raise the entire cloth. The clear message is that one person truly can make a difference in terms of improving the whole.

We might say that the consciousness of humankind can be compared to a scale, such as you find on a thermometer. Instead of temperature, the scale of consciousness measures people's level of self-knowledge, meaning how far they have sunk into separation or how close they are to oneness with their source. As an example we might say that the lowest people on earth, the people who are the most selfish, are at a consciousness level of minus 30. The people with the highest level of awareness are at plus 70, meaning that the range of consciousness is 100. Planet earth has a fixed span in terms of the range of consciousness that is allowed. Let us imagine that the people with the highest level of awareness discover and follow the spiritual path and attain a higher degree of oneness with all life whereby their consciousness is raised to 80. Because the range in consciousness cannot be more than 100, this will raise the bottom level of acceptable consciousness to minus 20.

The people with the lowest level of consciousness are now forced to make a choice. One option is that they choose to raise their consciousness and grow along with the rest of humanity. If they refuse to do that, they simply cannot remain on planet earth but will be reassigned to other "places" where the level of consciousness is lower. This is the inner meaning of my statements about the judgment, statements that have been widely misunderstood by fear-based preachers. Take my statement:

> 26 For as the Father hath life in himself; so hath he given to the Son to have life in himself;
> 27 And hath given him authority to execute judgment also, because he is the Son of man. (John, Chapter 5)

7 | Who Can Stop Religious Conflict?

As I said earlier, it is the Christ consciousness that determines who is saved. Likewise it is the Christ consciousness who determines who is allowed to stay on earth and who must descend to a lower realm:

> And Jesus said, For judgment I am come into this world, that they which see not might see; and that they which see might be made blind. (John 9:39)

Again, people are judged according to their level of Christ consciousness. If a critical mass of people raise their level of Christ consciousness, they raise the bar in terms of the lowest state of consciousness that is allowed on this planet. Those who refuse to raise their consciousness can no longer sit on the fence. They must follow the call to "choose you this day whom ye will serve" (Joshua 24:15). They must either choose the life of growth or the death of refusing to grow. If they choose death, they will be removed from the earth by the power of the ascended masters.

Can you give a practical example of how a trail blazed in the collective consciousness has led to a positive change in society?

There are literally thousands of such examples, but one particularly obvious one is the abolishment of slavery. For thousands of years, slavery was an accepted part of the culture in most civilizations. During the early 1800s, most nations decided to abolish it through national and international laws. Why did this happen? Some scientists claim that everything in human society is decided by economic factors. There was no economic incentive for abolishing slavery. If you owned slaves, you could have them produce goods – for a very low cost – that you could sell with a high profit. What was the incentive to give up that privilege?

Obviously, you can point to many outer factors that all played a part in the abolishment of slavery. However, the true spiritual reason was that the top ten percent of the people on earth had raised their sense of oneness with life to the point where it became unacceptable to them that a human being could be owned as a piece of property. Through the force of their consciousness, they pulled the general population up with them. Given that political leaders are exponents of the consciousness of their subjects, slavery was abolished. This is an obvious example of the immense power of a few people raising their consciousness and pulling the rest of humanity up with them.

However, it is important for people to understand the deeper truth in this matter. The reality is that God has given humankind free will, and it is up to people to determine what they will allow on this planet. God has the power to instantly remove all suffering and all darkness from earth. God has suspended that power and made it dependent upon the choices made by humankind.

If the top ten percent of the people on earth accept the existence of slavery, God will do nothing to remove it. The moment the top ten percent decide that slavery simply isn't acceptable, then God can take action. The first action is to present the lowest ten percent – the people who initiated slavery – with the judgment that forces them to make a choice. They must either choose to abolish slavery or be removed from the earth. Either way, humankind is set free from the downward pull of these people, and thus humankind is set free to abolish slavery. You will see this mechanism at work in all areas of society. How do you think democracy was established? Why do you think the feudal lords in Europe suddenly lost their power and their privileged positions, in many countries without a shot being fired?

The other side of the coin is that as long as the top ten percent continue to tolerate a certain problem, that problem will remain. For example, the top ten percent have not yet decided that it is unacceptable to them that millions of children die from starvation every year. To return to the topic at hand, they have not yet decided that religious conflict and warfare is unacceptable to them. If religious conflict is to vanish from the earth, the top ten percent must come to a firm decision that they simply will no longer tolerate the existence of religious conflict and the forces and beliefs that generate it. To reach that point, they must be willing to remove the beam in their own eyes by overcoming the consciousness of separation, which – as I have attempted to explain – is the real cause of religious conflict.

Is that why you said: "Thou hypocrite, first cast out the beam out of thine own eye; and then shalt thou see clearly to cast out the mote out of thy brother's eye" (Matthew 7:5)?

Correct. My statement applies to all human beings, but it has a special significance for the top ten percent. Although these people have a higher level of consciousness than the general population, they can often be misled into a form of finger pointing. For example, many spiritually mature people look at some of the hellfire and brimstone preachers who are screaming that all nonbelievers will burn forever in hell, and they feel they could never do something like that. Then they look at some of the Islamic fundamentalists blowing people up in the name of Allah, and they think they could never do something like that. They are right, yet because they would not take such extreme actions, they feel they have a high degree of religious tolerance. They reason that they are not contributing to the problem of religious conflict.

In reality, although these people would never actually carry out acts of religious intolerance, they have not overcome the consciousness of separation that leads to religious intolerance. While these people think they are not contributing to intolerance, they are actually doing so. Because they have the highest level of awareness, their influence on the general population is very powerful.

I don't mean to point the finger at any group, but let me give you one example. Many of the most advanced people on this planet can clearly see some of the fallacies of organized or orthodox religion. Many of these people were sorely disappointed by the religion in which they grew up, and in most cases they had perfectly valid reasons for this disappointment. Many of them took this disappointment too far by rejecting all religion, often even to the point of embracing scientific materialism and denying their own spirituality. These people have only gone from one extreme – blind faith in a particular religion – to the opposite extreme, namely blind rejection of all religion.

I am not saying this reaction isn't understandable, but as a lifestream matures and reaches a higher level of Christ consciousness, it begins to realize that these two reactions, either blindly following or blindly rejecting, are both expressions of the consciousness of duality that creates two relative opposites. The medieval Church was clearly too closed-minded, as seen by many open-minded people back then and today. Scientific materialism – which denies the existence of God and people's spiritual nature – is merely the opposite extreme of the orthodox approach to religion. Scientific materialism has not taken people out of duality; it has merely trapped them in a different form of duality than the one promoted by the Catholic Church.

The more mature reaction is to say that there is a different way to look at the problem than what is promoted by either of the two extremes. When you look at the problem of religious conflict from the perspective of the Christ mind, you see that the real cause is the sense of separation from your spiritual source. By using the fallacies of orthodox religion to abandon all spirituality and deny your own spiritual nature, you have done nothing to raise the consciousness of humankind out of duality. Many of the people who look with dismay upon fanatical religious people are still not part of the solution—they are part of the problem.

I can't honestly say that I have overcome the consciousness that leads to religious intolerance. It is an amazing thought that the people who are not doing the outer actions of religious intolerance can still contribute to the problem! Can you elaborate on that because it seems to be a really important point that I think most people overlook.

For starters, look at what you said earlier where you were so focused on the people who – admittedly – instigate religious conflict. You were reasoning that the only way to overcome conflict was to change their minds, and you were very concerned because you – correctly – see that their minds are completely closed. By being so focused on changing others, you are actually revealing that you are still somewhat blinded by the illusion of separation. You are – without seeing it – reinforcing this illusion by "identifying" the problem as being out there in the "others" and thus indirectly thinking there is nothing you can do to remove the problem.

When you understand what I have said about all people being connected in consciousness, you gain a deeper perspective on my statement to first pull the beam from your own eye. The illusion of separation – exploited by the lowest ten percent of the manipulators – has caused people to always seek to change others. In reality, the most powerful way to change the world is to change yourself and go all the way to the Christ consciousness. According to the Law of Free Will you have no right to change the mind of others. You also have no obligation to hold back your own growth to accommodate others and their unwillingness to change. By making full use of your ability to raise your individual consciousness to the Christic level, you will generate a very powerful force that will inevitably "force" others to choose between life and death.

The consciousness of wanting to change the minds of other people is something that the most spiritual people need to leave behind? I mean, all of my life I have thought I needed to convert other people to see the spiritual side of life.

Let us try to step back from the issue and consider how religious conflict could possibly be removed from the earth. Or rather, let us consider which people are most likely to remove religious conflict.

It is easy to identify the people who are actually carrying out religious warfare or acts of intolerance. Almost every religion has certain elements that are extremist, fanatical or fundamentalist. They believe their religion is the only true one and that all other religions are false teachings spread by the devil. Since the devil is the ultimate source of evil, these people think it is acceptable for them to kill those who represent the devil. They think that even if such acts violate God's command not to kill, they will still further God's plan for a better earth. Unfortunately, Christianity is not free from this way of thinking. It wasn't that long ago that Protestants and Catholics killed each other in Northern Ireland, and more recently certain Christian forces in the United States had a major influence on the mindset behind the Iraq war.

It would be easy to look at these religious extremists and say that they are the cause of religious conflict. This is a very superficial way of reasoning, which becomes obvious as soon as you start looking at the logical consequences. If you identify religious extremists as the only cause of religious conflict, it follows logically that the only option for removing conflict is to change the religious extremists.

People who fall into the consciousness of religious extremism are some of the most closed-minded people you could ever meet. Believe me, I was up against such people in the form of the scribes and Pharisees. These people have closed their minds to such a degree that there is literally nothing you could say that would change their approach to religion. Let us imagine that the more moderate people on earth decided to create a task force to remove religious conflict. They soon identified the extremists as the cause, and they engaged in a well-meant attempt to persuade these people about the folly of their ways. After a valiant effort, the task force was forced to admit that they had gotten absolutely nowhere. Despite all of the perfectly sensible arguments – arguments that are sensible to people who are not extremists – they had not managed to persuade the extremists to beat their swords into plowshares.

The task force would now be faced with two options. It could admit that it was completely powerless to do anything about the problem and give up. Or it could seek to use governments to combat religious intolerance through force. A free democratic government cannot eradicate fanaticism through force. The reason being that such a government is not prepared to take the step of imprisoning, killing or deporting all religious extremists.

If you cannot combat conflict by persuading the religious extremists, your only option is to eradicate extremism through force. By doing so, you only contribute to the sense of separation that caused the religious intolerance in the first place. You now cross the same line already crossed by the extremists, namely saying that the ends can justify the means. You become part of the problem instead of the solution. Is there another way to look at the problem? There is, and let me start with another quote:

> But I say unto you, That ye resist not evil: but whosoever shall smite thee on thy right cheek, turn to him the other also. (Matthew 5:39)

The inner meaning of this quote is that you cannot combat evil through force. If you try, you inevitably enter into the dualistic consciousness of evil, and you become part of evil. You form an opposite polarity to a particular expression of evil, and thereby you reinforce the duality consciousness, which is the very basis for the existence of evil. The only way to combat evil is to stay free of the consciousness of evil, the consciousness of duality and separation.

Again, let us imagine that the top ten percent of the people on earth decided that they wanted to remove religious conflict. They cannot persuade the religious extremists so they can either admit that they are powerless or they can use force, and in either case they become part of the problem. These are not the only options. The alternative is to look at the problem through the mind of Christ, which I described in this quote:

> The light of the body is the eye: if therefore thine eye be single, thy whole body shall be full of light. (Matthew 6:22)

The inner meaning is that when your vision is single – when you no longer look at a problem through the filter of duality – you will see the problem in the light of oneness. In that light, the solution becomes obvious. In this case, the reality is that it is quite possible to remove religious conflict without persuading or exterminating the religious extremists. The solution is that the top ten percent of the people look at the beam in their own eyes – the consciousness of separation and duality – and decide to remove it.

When they have successfully raised their own consciousness beyond the level that leads to religious conflict and intolerance, they can then make the decision – individually or collectively – that religious conflict is no longer acceptable on this planet. At that point, they will give God the authority to step into the picture and force the religious extremists to either abandon their extremism or be removed from the earth. Either way, the problem will be solved, and it will be solved because the top ten percent of the people have raised the bar for the level of consciousness that is acceptable on this planet.

If you are willing to change yourself – to remove the beam in your own eye – you are never powerless. You are on your way to being given all power in heaven and on earth (Matthew 28:18). This does not mean that you have the right to violate the free will of others. But it does mean that your mind is no longer a house divided against itself (Mark 3:25), and therefore you know that your lifestream is one with your spiritual self. You can be here on earth the spiritual being that you truly are in the spiritual realm, meaning that you have maximum power to pull on the collective consciousness. This does not force others, but it makes it easier for them to make better choices.

The other side of the coin is that the lowest ten percent of the people can pull the general population down, just as the top ten percent can pull them up?

Correct, and that is the true meaning of the saying: "For evil to triumph, it only takes that good men – and women – do nothing." Again, it is extremely unlikely that the people with the lowest state of consciousness will change of their own accord. They will continue to do what they are doing until they are faced with the judgment. They will always seek to pull the general population down in order to control society. If the top ten percent do nothing to counteract the downward pull of the lowest ten percent, evil will truly triumph. Only, it will be a short-lived triumph because the forces of evil will inevitably self-destruct. Unfortunately, they could potentially destroy the rest of humankind and even the entire planet in the process.

When you look at some of the worst atrocities in history, you will see that they were caused by the lowest ten percent, yet they happened only because the top ten percent did nothing to counteract it. The top ten percent had not removed the beam in their own eyes, and they could not make the firm decision that this or that evil was not acceptable on earth. In some cases people from the top ten percent were pulled into a dualistic struggle between two opposing forces, and they contributed to the consciousness of duality and separation.

Even today there are many examples of how the top ten percent are still so blinded by dualistic beliefs that they cannot counteract the downward pull of the lowest ten percent. The top ten percent have not yet decided that poverty, starvation, pornography, sexual exploitation, abuse of children, genocide, terrorism, nuclear weapons, pollution, drug abuse, manipulation of oil prices, dependency on oil for energy and a host of other problems are unacceptable on this planet. That is why these problems are still around.

Because the top ten percent have a higher level of awareness, they can relatively easily counteract the lowest ten percent. However, to do so they must stop being a house divided against itself, and this can happen only when people go beyond a dualistic view of a problem and allow their vision to become single through the mind of Christ. Only then can the power of God work through them and solve the problem.

I am intrigued by the idea that we can think we are fighting for a good cause yet we are only reinforcing the duality consciousness, and thus we are helping evil grow. Can you give an example of that from history?

There are thousands of examples, yet the most obvious – and in this context relevant – one is the war between orthodox religion and materialistic science. The medieval Catholic Church perpetrated the Crusades and the Inquisition so any objective person must conclude that the Church had been heavily influenced by the consciousness of separation and duality. The very church that claimed to be the only true representative of Christ on earth was in reality dominated by the consciousness of anti-christ.

I can see many Catholics objecting vehemently.

Yes, but as I said, any objective person must accept the indisputable historical evidence. In medieval times, the Catholic Church was clearly attempting to prevent people from knowing basic facts when those facts contradicted Catholic doctrine. The Church has changed somewhat since then, but no sane person can deny the dark past. The only possible conclusion is that the Church was influenced by the duality consciousness. You don't seriously believe that I told the Pope to torture people, do you?

The early scientists were persecuted by the Church, and the result was a conflict between the Church and science. In reality, this conflict was completely unnecessary. However, its appearance was not exclusively the fault of Catholics. The sad fact is that, as science gained more power, many scientists began to look at the Church – and all religion – as the enemy of science. In so doing, they defined science as the opposite polarity to the Church, and they believed it was the just cause of science to free people from the superstitions promoted by the Church. They developed scientific materialism that denies the existence of God and the spiritual aspects of human nature.

What these scientists overlooked was that the Church had taken the duality consciousness into one extreme, and by positioning science in opposition to the Church, science was taken into the opposite extreme. Even though both sides clearly had some true ideas, neither the Church nor science was promoting an approach to life that reaches beyond duality. Each side promoted a dualistic, relative approach to life that defined truth and attempted to force reality to conform to man-made doctrines and theories. The Catholic Church promoted the doctrine that there is only one true religion, and materialistic science promoted the concept that there is no true religion. Both ideas clearly spring from the consciousness of separation from God. The net result of the war between mainstream Christianity and materialistic science is that humankind has become progressively more polarized. None of the two polarities represent a non-dualistic truth, despite the claims made

7 | Who Can Stop Religious Conflict?

by both sides. The only way out is that the top ten percent begin to see the futility of this dualistic struggle so they can stop giving their support to one of the two sides. When you are trapped in duality, you think in terms of black and white so you think that either Christianity or science must be right. The only solution to the conflict is that one side wins and eradicates the other side.

From the higher perspective of the Christ mind, you see the situation differently. You clearly see that both sides are promoting a dualistic belief system so both of them are not right in a higher sense. The true solution is that humankind must raise its consciousness so people can see beyond the two dualistic extremes. It is not a matter of science eradicating religion or religion eradicating science. The true solution is that humankind is raised above the consciousness of duality and finds a better approach to life. This approach will incorporate many of the findings of science, yet it will not deny the existence of God or the fact that human beings do have a spiritual nature. We might say that the Christ solution to a conflict is to transcend both of the dualistic extremes that created the conflict. By doing so, you replace the relative beliefs with a higher understanding based on unity. You cannot remove conflict through force; the only way to truly remove conflict is through self-transcendence.

I foresee that many people will not be willing to accept this idea. They will cling to their dualistic belief systems.

Which is precisely why only the top ten percent of the people can remove religious conflict. The people in the top ten percent should be able and willing – after some honest contemplation – to accept the Christ solution to conflict.

What exactly can people in the top ten percent do to make their personal contribution?

They have to walk the path that leads them out of the dualistic state of consciousness and into the higher state of consciousness, whether you call it the Christ consciousness, the Buddha consciousness or something else. This is what I earlier called the spiritual path, and as I said, all religions are meant to describe that universal path in a way that is suited for a particular group of people.

When a person reaches a high level of spiritual awareness, he or she can walk that path based on inner direction. For most people, it will be helpful to follow some kind of spiritual teaching. You can find such teachings by looking at the spiritual, inner or mystical aspects of any of the major world religions. You can also find a variety of teachings that are not tied to a traditional religion. Such teachings are often labeled "New Age" by orthodox religions, but some of them are truly universal and can be followed by anyone, even those who have abandoned all organized or traditional religion.

The specifics of how to walk the spiritual path go beyond what we can cover in this book, and they do depend on which outer teaching you choose as your onramp to the spiritual path. You can find many books that describe the universal path. I have described that path in the previous books in this series, in other books and on our websites.

You have said that we need to attain a sense of oneness with all life, yet you have now divided humanity into three categories. Aren't you concerned that people can use your model of consciousness to reason that they belong to the top ten percent and thus it is their duty to fight the lowest ten percent?

As long as people are trapped in the duality consciousness, they will use any type of distinction as an excuse for defining an enemy and setting up a struggle between two sides. People in this state of consciousness have already defined enemies, and they are not likely to read this book. My scale of consciousness will not do much to increase the totality of conflict.

By dividing humanity into categories based on their level of consciousness, we gain a tool that can be helpful to the top ten percent. The top ten percent can remove conflict only by removing the beam in their own eyes and transcending the duality consciousness. As they do so, they will overcome the need to define other people as enemies. They will realize that a Christed being is never fighting against other people. At the lower levels of Christ consciousness, you might be fighting against specific ideas and against the entire duality consciousness. As you climb higher, you stop fighting against anything. Instead, you begin to fight for truth instead of fighting against error. Your focus shifts away from dualistic imperfections until you attain the single vision of the Christ mind in which you see only God's perfection. You are no longer working to remove error, you are working to spread truth. Your "weapon" is to give people the truth that will make them free (John 8:32). Your sword of truth is always wielded with unconditional love, the perfect love that will cast out all fear in yourself and others (1John 4:18).

8 | A NONVIOLENT APPROACH TO MYSTICAL VISIONS

I realize we can't go into detail about following the spiritual path and that the previous books in this series have done so. After over 30 years of walking the mystical path and interacting with a wide variety of spiritually open-minded people, I do foresee some hurdles. For example, I have observed that even those who are willing to go beyond traditional and fundamentalist religions can fall prey to the idea that their teaching or organization is the only true or the best one. I also see some people who are very suspicious about teachings from other sources, and I see some people who have a need to believe they are the only ones saving the world. I would like to talk about some of the things that the top ten percent need to overcome, and I would like to begin by asking you about spiritual visions.

You said earlier that truth cannot be expressed in words, but that it must be experienced through an intuitive, spiritual or mystical vision. One of the keys to overcoming religious

> conflict is that more people attain spiritual experiences or visions. You have said that, in this age, it is becoming easier for people to have such visions. If we look at history, we see that many people have had spiritual visions, and in many cases they were different. In some cases two people had visions that were either mutually exclusive or were interpreted as being in conflict. How can people deal with that problem?

Let me begin by explaining the key to walking the spiritual path. We earlier talked about the fact that most people have lost the direct connection to their source, to the spiritual realm. When a person has that connection, it knows it is more than a human being. It knows that the core of its being is a self that is beyond any identity in this world. In the previous books I have called this the pure self or the Conscious You. The person knows it is an extension of a greater whole, and we might call it the spiritual self. This spiritual self permanently resides in the spiritual realm and it cannot be affected or damaged by anything you experience in this world. When a person has a conscious connection to its spiritual self, it will identify itself as an immortal spiritual being, as a son or daughter of God.

When a person loses its conscious connection to the spiritual self, it loses its sense of identity as a spiritual being. The Conscious You cannot exist in a vacuum, and it simply cannot bear to exist without a sense of identity. The Conscious You must create a new sense of identity, and it creates a new self that becomes a replacement for the spiritual self. This new self, this pseudo self, is what some modern psychologists and some spiritual teachings call the human ego.

The ego owes its existence to the Conscious You's sense of separation from the spiritual self. The ego is born out of separation and duality. To the ego, everything is relative, and the ego can always create a mental image or interpretation that makes it seem like it is right. The ego can – in its own mind – never be proven wrong. If the Conscious You believes in the illusions created by the ego, it will quickly become stuck in the belief that its mental images are completely correct and represent an absolute truth. The Conscious You is lost in a net of dualistic illusions that ties it to this world and the consciousness of this world. The prince of this world (John 14:30), meaning the consciousness of duality, has something in the soul and is using it to control the Conscious You.

The essence of the spiritual path is that the Conscious You must be willing to leave its nets of entanglements with the duality of the ego and follow a higher vision, namely the unified vision of the Christ mind. The Conscious You must be willing to leave behind the consciousness of duality and become a disciple of the Christ mind. It must be reborn into a true sense of identity as a spiritual being, thereby realizing that the ego can indeed be wrong. The Conscious You can then begin to accept a higher understanding of life that allows it to see when and how the ego's mental images are out of alignment with God's truth. One might say that the Conscious You must stop dancing around the golden calf created by the ego and be willing to ascend the mountain of God to receive a truth that is not dualistic and relative. By following the spiritual path, a person can gradually put off the old human – the dualistic sense of identity based on the illusions of the ego – and put on a new sense of identity as a spiritual being. One might say that the essence of the spiritual path is to overcome the ego and free the Conscious You from all mental images and illusions.

This is where many spiritual seekers get sidetracked. They often subscribe to the idea that if only they follow a particular spiritual teaching or guru, belong to the right organization or perform a certain spiritual technique, they will automatically overcome the ego, and one day they will wake up as enlightened beings. In reality, there is no such outer or automatic salvation, and that is why I said that your righteousness must exceed the righteousness of the scribes and Pharisees (Matthew 5:20). That is also why the Old Testament says:

> There is a way which seemeth right unto a man, but the end thereof are the ways of death. (Proverbs 14:12)

The true path to salvation is a path through which the Conscious You begins to actively see through the illusions created by its own ego and by the collective consciousness of humankind. As I have said, God has given every Conscious You free will. Sometime in the past, a Conscious You made the decision to accept a certain illusion, and the illusion became a part of the soul vehicle, the person's sense of identity. No being in the spiritual realm and no spiritual teacher on earth can undo the Conscious You's decision. The Conscious You must do so itself by using its free will. However, to replace the limited choice from the past, the Conscious You must first see through the illusion that caused it to make that decision. Only then can it replace the old decision with a better decision.

Following the spiritual path is not a matter of stepping onto a train, leaning back and allowing the train to take you to the destination. The path is like walking a road that has many forks. At each fork, you must make a decision and the essence of each decision is whether you will continue to affirm one of the ego's illusions or whether you will – finally – see through that illusion and choose to leave it behind. If the top ten percent of the people on earth are to overcome the consciousness that leads to religious conflict, they have to consciously see through the ego-illusions that make up this mindset. People need to become aware of how the illusions of their egos affect their approach to religion.

Can you help us see how the ego affects spiritual visions?

Certainly, and the first step must be to recognize that the ego is born of duality, which means that it always thinks in terms of two relative opposites, it thinks in terms of black and white. For example, to the ego a spiritual teaching or vision must be either true or false, meaning that if two spiritual visions differ, one must be true and the other false. This quickly leads the members of a particular religion or spiritual organization to reason that since their religion must be true, any vision or teaching that is different from their own must be false. That is to say, they will reason this way if they are still trapped by their egos.

As you become a more mature spiritual seeker, you need to realize that there are a number of reasons why spiritual visions can be different and still be valid. To explain this, let us start with a logical question. When two people have a spiritual vision, do they necessarily have to see the same thing? Imagine that a medieval king sent two explorers to North America and one landed on the rocky coast of Maine whereas the other landed on the sandy beaches of Florida. They came back with different descriptions, but do we have to say that one had the true vision of America and the other is a charlatan?

Let us revisit the fact that everything is made of energy. Science has difficulty defining energy and often describes it as a form of vibration. For example, visible light is energy that vibrates within a certain spectrum of frequencies. You know there are forms of light, such as ultraviolet and X-rays, that your eyes cannot see. All modern people should be open to the possibility that there could be forms of energy, levels of vibration, beyond those found in the material universe.

We might say that the material universe is made of energy that vibrates within a certain frequency spectrum and beyond that spectrum are energies of a higher vibration. These higher energies are what religious people have traditionally called heaven, but I prefer to call them the spiritual realm. While you are still trapped in the consciousness of separation, you think heaven is far above the material universe, and there is an impenetrable barrier between heaven and earth. This is the thinking of many orthodox or fundamentalist religious people.

When you begin to overcome duality, you see that the spiritual realm is made of the same kind of energy as the material universe, the only difference being that the energies in the spiritual realm vibrate at a higher rate. In reality, everything is made from the same substance, whether we call it energy or God's consciousness, and there are no impenetrable barriers. The spiritual realm is co-existing with the material world in the same "space," although it is not a material space. That is why the kingdom of God is within you, which is the realization of all mystics. It is this fact that makes it possible for a Conscious You in a physical body to have a vision of the spiritual realm. If there was an impenetrable barrier, no person could have such visions and there could be no communication from the spiritual realm to earth, meaning there would be no true religion. If there was a barrier between heaven and earth, no being in the spiritual realm could give a spiritual teaching to human beings, meaning that all religion would be man-made. There would be no hope of ever resolving religious conflict.

When you accept the fact that there are different levels of vibration, it becomes easy to see that just as there are several levels of vibration in the material universe (for example, the colors of the rainbow are light rays of different frequencies), there are several levels in the spiritual realm. We might talk about a number of octaves like you find on the tonal scale. If you go beyond the vibrations of the material universe, you encounter a spectrum of higher vibrations. We might call this the lower spiritual realm. As you keep going toward higher vibrations, you enter higher levels of the spiritual world. The Bible actually supports this view because I said that my father's house has many mansions (John 14:2). There are several levels of the spiritual realm and they are somewhat different.

Let us now consider why people can have a spiritual experience. The reason is that the Conscious You has the ability to act like a radio receiver. As you can tune the radio to different frequencies, or stations, you can tune the Conscious You to different levels of vibration. The Conscious You can reach beyond the material world and tune in to vibrations that are different from those of the material universe. That is why some people have had visions of heaven, while others have had visions of hell. When people have a spiritual vision, the simplest explanation is to say that they have turned the dial of consciousness and tuned in to one of the levels in the spiritual realm. When you realize that there is more than one level in the spiritual world, you see that different people might tune in to different levels. If two people tune in to two different levels of the spiritual realm, they will have different visions. It is perfectly possible that two people can have different spiritual visions and they can both be valid visions.

Is there a connection between people's background, such as their religion, and the kind of visions they are likely to have?

Certainly. If you look at the visions of the spiritual realm given by different religions, the truth is that most of them are correct in the sense that there really is a "place" in the spiritual realm that looks similar to the Hindu heaven and there is another place looking much like the Christian heaven. The same holds true for many other religions, small or large. My only note of caution is that some religions have been so affected by the consciousness of duality that they have distorted the original vision of the spiritual realm given to that religion.

When a person grows up in a particular religious culture, he or she naturally absorbs that religion's vision of heaven. The person's mind is saturated with that vision, and this has the effect of attuning the dial in the person's mind to the particular "station" in the spiritual realm that formed the basis for the person's religion. When such a person has a spiritual vision, it is only natural that he or she will see a particular place in the spiritual realm. The person's vision will seem to confirm the outer religion.

The core of the problem is that when a person has a spiritual vision, that vision seems extremely real. People often fail to understand that what gives this sense of ultimate realism is their contact with a level of reality that is beyond the duality and relativity of the ego. The sense of realism does not come from the form or content of the vision. It comes from making contact with the mind of Christ, which is the key of knowledge, the key to experiencing God's reality as opposed to the ego's dualistic "reality."

When a Catholic has a spiritual vision, the vision often conforms to the person's core beliefs, and they conform to the outer doctrines of the Church. The same happens when a Hindu or a Muslim has a spiritual vision. You now have different people with different visions, each of whom has experienced the supreme realism of the higher state of consciousness. If these people do not understand what I have just explained, it is inevitable that each person feels that his or her vision is

8 | A Nonviolent Approach to Mystical Visions

absolutely true. All conflicting visions must be false. If a person is still partially trapped in the consciousness of the ego, the person might use a spiritual vision to fuel religious conflict. This, of course, is in complete opposition to the true purpose of spiritual visions.

I am still wondering why the visions of the spiritual realm given by different religions are so different. Is there a connection between people's level of consciousness and the vision of heaven they were given in their religion?

Different religions were given to people in different cultures. When the ascended masters gave the target audience a particular religious teaching, we had to use images and metaphors that people could grasp with the level of consciousness and the cultural background they had at the time. Two religions can have different descriptions of the spiritual realm because they refer to two different levels of the spiritual world and because they were given to people in different states of consciousness.

When you realize this, you can quickly rise to the more mature understanding that the Hindu description of heaven is not in conflict with the Christian description of heaven. The purpose of both religions is to raise people out of the consciousness of duality, and that can happen only when people are willing to look beyond the outer religion. If people become emotionally attached to the outer description of the spiritual realm and begin to use it as a weapon against the members of other religions, they are misusing their own religion, and this stems from the ego. They are literally using their religion – which was given in order to set them free from the ego – to bury their souls even more deeply in the consciousness of duality. To be more direct, one might say that a Hindu should focus on entering the Hindu heaven and let a Christian focus on entering the Christian heaven—and the other way around. Once they are both in their respective heavens, they have both escaped the consciousness of duality, which is the whole point.

When people do not understand this dynamic, they often return from a spiritual vision thinking that the vision confirmed all of their current beliefs. Because the vision seemed so real, they feel they received an undeniable and unquestionable proof that their particular religious doctrine and belief is the absolute truth. When you understand that people's beliefs can influence their vision, you see that this is not necessarily a correct line of reasoning.

We have said that there are different "places" in the spiritual realm and different people can have different visions. Are you now saying that even while a vision is taking place, the vision can be affected by people's beliefs? You could have two people who saw the same place in the spiritual realm yet they would have slightly different visions?

That is correct. You have no doubt heard about a situation often encountered by law enforcement personnel, namely that five people witness an accident and give five different descriptions of what happened. The five people witnessed the exact same event so what can explain the different descriptions? In the end, you have to recognize that each person's view of the event was influenced by the person's consciousness. As an illustration of this, look at the following quote:

> For now we see through a glass, darkly; but then face to face: now I know in part; but then shall I know even as also I am known. (1Corinthians, 13:12)

Paul was well aware that while you are still influenced by the ego, you cannot have a completely pure spiritual vision. You will see through a glass darkly, meaning that you see through the colored glass of the dualistic beliefs of your ego. A person can have a vision that is genuine in the sense that the vision does show the person something that is beyond the material realm. The vision might not be completely pure, meaning that it can – in subtle ways – be affected by the person's consciousness. This is in perfect accord with the findings of quantum physics, as mentioned earlier. The essence of these findings is that when a scientist observes a subatomic particle, the results of the observation are the products of what is called the "entire measurement situation." This involves three elements, namely the subatomic "entity," the scientific instrument used and the consciousness of the scientist. When you have a spiritual vision, you have a more simple situation in that you have no mechanical instrument. You have, so to speak, cut out the middleman. The vision will still be a product of the entire measurement situation, which involves a particular level of the spiritual realm and the consciousness of the observer. There is simply no way to have a spiritual vision that is not somewhat affected by your consciousness because it is through your consciousness that you have the vision. The only question is how your consciousness affects the vision.

I think a lot of spiritual people have the impression that if you have a spiritual vision, it must mean that you are an advanced soul. You must have a high level of spiritual maturity, a high level of Christ consciousness. Are you saying that is not the case?

What do you think I meant when I said: "The kingdom of heaven suffereth violence, and the violent take it by force"

(Matthew 11:12)? Some people decide that they want to have a spiritual vision, yet they are not willing to relinquish the ego and rise above the consciousness of duality. They are not willing to follow a gradual path whereby they earn a vision. Instead, they want instant gratification so they look for ways to force a spiritual vision, and some people use drugs or certain spiritual techniques to accomplish this goal.

The key to having a spiritual vision is to turn the dial of consciousness, and most people are able to do that. For example, most people can get drunk, which makes them experience a different state of consciousness. When you turn the dial of the mind, you will experience something that is beyond your normal state of awareness, yet which station do you get in on the radio? If people are deeply enmeshed in the consciousness of duality, they can still turn the dial, but they will often tune in to a level of reality that is below the spiritual realm. There are certain levels of energies below the spiritual realm, and they are often called the psychic realm. Some of these levels resemble the heaven world, while others look like hell.

If a person is not completely trapped in duality, that person might have a vision of the spiritual realm. The vision is seen through a filter, namely the person's remaining dualistic beliefs. As one example of how your current beliefs can influence a spiritual vision, let us look at the fact that many people have had a near-death experience in which I came to greet them after they went through the tunnel. Several people have reported having different visions of Jesus Christ. In some cases, a person's vision conformed to a painting or sculpture that the person liked while alive. When you look at this situation through the duality of the lower mind, you tend to reason that there can be only one Jesus Christ, and therefore I should always look the same. If people have different visions of me, some of those visions must be false. The truth is that a person's mind can impose a preconceived image upon the spiritual vision. This does not mean that the vision is invalid – because the person did go beyond the consciousness of duality – but it does mean that it is not a pure vision.

Another reason visions differ is the fact that we of the ascended masters are constantly trying to raise people's level of consciousness, and in order to do that we must first make contact with people. To make contact with people, we must approach them in a way they can accept. For example, when a person dies and the person's lifestream enters the spiritual realm, the Conscious You is often somewhat shocked and feels distraught. When I approach such a lifestream, my first and foremost concern is to make it feel at peace in its new circumstance. If the lifestream has a strong devotion to a particular image of me, I will appear in the form of that image. In the spiritual realm things are much more fluid than they are on earth. I can change my appearance in a variety of ways. However, in some instances I do not have to change my appearance because people have such a strong mental image of me that they literally impose that image upon my Presence. They are not able to see beyond the image.

To return to your question, the true measure of spiritual attainment is not spiritual visions. The true measure is what level of consciousness the person is able to maintain during his or her daily activities. Can you maintain a high level of oneness with your source, oneness with all life, so that you treat people with love and avoid responding to situations with fear?

Can you tell us more about how perception works?

Your Conscious You was originally created as an extension of your spiritual self. The reality is that everything was created from God's energy. We might say everything is upheld by a flow of energy that originates with God and flows through the many levels of vibration that make up the world of form. We might say that God's pure light is gradually lowered in vibration until it reaches the vibratory level of the material universe.

In your individual lifestream, the flow of energy originates in your spiritual self and then flows into the Conscious You and then into your soul vehicle (what we in previous books described as the four levels of the mind or your four lower bodies). Your soul vehicle remains alive because it is constantly receiving a stream of energy from your spiritual self. As that stream of energy descends into the soul, it first hits your sense of identity. Your sense of identity forms a filter through which the light must pass.

An illustration of this would be a kaleidoscope. The colored glass pieces inside the kaleidoscope represent the dualistic ideas and beliefs that you have accepted as part of your identity. As you know, the glass pieces inside a kaleidoscope will color light flowing through the device. If you put enough glass pieces inside a kaleidoscope, you cannot see the white light that enters at one end. You only see light that is colored by the glass pieces.

Only after the light from your spiritual self has passed through the kaleidoscope of your sense of identity will that light be "visible" to your conscious mind. In passing through the kaleidoscope of self, the light is colored by your beliefs. You no longer see God's absolute truth, you see a relative "truth" colored by the mental images in your consciousness. The result is that when you make a decision, you are not basing it on the truth of God; you are basing it on a relative truth colored by your ego. This can severely limit your ability to make free, conscious choices about what you want to think, what you want to feel and what you want to do. One might say that your ego programs your mind to think, feel and act in certain ways. If you only look at a person's outer actions, those actions can be difficult to explain. When you apply the model I have just outlined, you gain a different perspective. Everything a person does is done with energy from the spiritual self. When that energy enters the material realm, it is colored by the contents of the kaleidoscope of self, meaning the ideas and beliefs that the Conscious You has made part of its sense of identity. By the time the energy flows into the part of the mind that makes conscious choices, the person is already predisposed to make choices within the framework that is defined by his or her sense of identity.

Another way to explain this would be to say that there are different layers, or levels, of the mind. The highest level of the mind stores your sense of identity and world view. What kind of individual does the Conscious You think it is? How does the Conscious You see the world and its relationship to God? Your sense of identity and world view act as a filter, and the Conscious You looks at everything through that filter. The level at which the Conscious You makes choices is below, and therefore subject to, its sense of identity. The consequence is that the Conscious You's choices will be affected by, they will be expressions of, your sense of identity. If you see yourself as a mortal human being, every choice you make is influenced by that self-image.

It is possible for your conscious mind to override your sense of identity and make a choice that is not affected by your subconscious mind. However, it is extremely difficult to do so. For most people, the vast majority of their choices are simply effects of their sense of identity. Most people's actions are not based on conscious, free choices that are made immediately before the action takes place. They spring from choices that were made a long time ago when the Conscious You accepted certain ideas as part of its sense of identity. As a visual example, let us use the fact that many people associate the color red with anger. Let us say that a person in the past accepted the belief that it is necessary or unavoidable to respond to certain situations with anger. The person put a number of red glass pieces into his or her kaleidoscope. As the light from the person's spiritual self passes through that kaleidoscope, it is colored red by the glass pieces. The person is therefore predisposed to respond to many situations with anger and cannot see any other way to respond. The person is not making a conscious choice to respond with anger because the choice was made when the Conscious You accepted certain beliefs about life. Such beliefs often cause a person to be angry – at subconscious levels – with itself, with other people and with God. All anger is anger against the self and ultimately against God.

This ego-driven mechanism explains much religious conflict. Many people have grown up in a religious culture that is dominated by duality and separation. In such a culture, the underlying feeling is fear, but in order to deal with the fear, people often use anger as a way to channel the fear away from themselves. They subscribe to the belief that they are threatened by other people. The real threat is their own egos, but their fear prevents them from acknowledging this beam in their own eyes. In order to avoid battling their internal demons, they "invent" an outer enemy who becomes the scapegoat. This can lead an entire culture to believe that the members of another religion are the ultimate threat to God's plan, and it is their duty to exterminate the enemies of God. Such a culture is often controlled by a few people, and I described them in the following saying:

> Beware of false prophets, which come to you in sheep's clothing, but inwardly they are ravening wolves. (Matthew 7:15)

The false prophets are those who claim to be religious people, but in reality they preach a gospel of separation, duality, fear, anger and hatred.

How do we get out of this jungle of dualistic illusions?

Let us look at what happens when a person discovers the spiritual path. Before a person can discover the path, it must have recognized the need to achieve a higher understanding of life. The person might find a particular religious or spiritual philosophy which offers a higher understanding in an outer form. However, when the person studies the outer teaching, it is not actually seeing the outer teaching. When the person is looking at the world, it is looking through the kaleidoscope of its sense of identity. What the person sees is not the spiritual teaching in its pure form but its own personal perception of the original teaching. The same, of course, holds true when such a person has a spiritual vision. Even if the person actually sees a level of the spiritual realm, the vision will be colored by the person's beliefs.

Anything the person experiences is experienced through, and therefore colored by, the kaleidoscope of identity. One might say that the person's sense of identity forms an image of the world, and the person is subconsciously projecting that image onto everything it encounters. The person does not see reality as it is; it sees reality through a kaleidoscope in which the person's core beliefs color its perception. If a person has accepted many dualistic ideas and beliefs, it will see a greatly distorted, possibly a completely false, image of reality.

There are two basic options. If a person is not willing to question its image of reality, it will use its religious teaching to solidify this image and the belief that the image represents an absolute truth. The person will literally use a religion – designed to bring it closer to oneness with God – to separate itself even more from God's truth. The person will then be as the people I described in the following quote:

> Can the blind lead the blind? Shall they not both fall into the ditch? (Luke 6:39)

If the person is willing to use the religious teaching as a stepping stone for a higher understanding that comes from within, it will gradually remove its false beliefs and replace them with knowledge. One might say that the person gradually removes the colored pieces of glass in the kaleidoscope of self. As a result of this process, the person achieves a more true and accurate view of reality, a view that is not colored by dualistic beliefs. It is extremely important to realize that as the person removes false or inaccurate beliefs, the Conscious You does not lose its individuality. What the Conscious You does lose is the pseudo individuality of the ego. Instead of this false individuality, the Conscious You now uncovers its God-given individuality. As this happens, the Conscious You begins to feel more whole, more happy, more fulfilled and more at peace. The Conscious You begins to feel that it knows itself, and it begins to accept itself as a worthy son or daughter of God. This point often confuses spiritual seekers. As you remove the false sense of identity, you will not end up in a vacuum. You will not end up with no sense of identity, with no personality or individuality. You will end up with your God-given individuality, which I can assure you is infinitely more beautiful and wonderful than the pseudo sense of identity you have built in the material world. Your true individuality is the pearl of great price. It has been covered over by many layers of the ego's illusions, and the essence of the spiritual path is to remove the layers of dualistic beliefs. As I said 2,000 years ago, the person who realizes the value of his or her true individuality, gladly sells everything to buy the pearl of great price (Matthew 13:45-46), meaning that the Conscious You gladly let's go of the pseudo identity. This is the idea expressed in my saying: "He who is willing to lose his life for my sake shall find it" (Matthew 16:25). He who is willing to lose the false sense of identity, the false sense of life created by the ego, shall find the true sense of identity, the eternal life, as a spiritual being.

I realize this was a very long explanation, but we can now see that until a person reaches the higher levels of the spiritual path and attains a high degree of Christ consciousness, the Conscious You still has numerous false ideas that color its perception of reality. This coloring extends to the person's spiritual visions. For example, you will see certain Catholic saints who had many spiritual visions. Those visions were valid visions, yet in some cases the visions never went beyond the person's core beliefs. For example, Padre Pio had many visions but to his dying day never questioned the Church's denial of reincarnation—even though his visions showed him that his soul could live independently of the body. It is quite possible that even an advanced lifestream can hold on to a dualistic belief, which the Conscious You is not yet ready to surrender. Even though the person can have many valid spiritual visions, the visions will not question that core belief. The Conscious You either will not be able to see anything in the spiritual world that goes beyond its core beliefs, or it will project those beliefs unto what it does see. The unfortunate result is that such a person might be firmly convinced that its spiritual visions affirm its core beliefs. This conviction will remain firm until the person reaches a higher level of consciousness, in which it is finally ready and willing to look beyond that particular belief.

If our egos can actually distort a spiritual vision while it is taking place, what does the ego do after the vision?

It depends on the person's willingness to change. A spiritual vision is always an opportunity for the person to discover a transcendental reality, meaning a reality beyond the person's current level of consciousness, a reality beyond the material world and a reality beyond the person's current beliefs and belief system. The core message of a spiritual vision is an opportunity for the Conscious You to come up higher in consciousness. However, to heed that message, the Conscious You must be willing to look beyond some of its existing beliefs, and the person might also have to make some changes to its lifestyle. If the Conscious You is not willing to truly change itself, it must find a way to impose a rationalization upon the spiritual vision. The Conscious You must make it seem like the vision conforms to – rather than challenges – its belief system.

You will see that some people have had a near-death experience or spiritual vision, and it completely turned their lives around. Others have had such experiences without making major changes, and such people often seek to fit the vision into the context of their current belief system. For example, if a Catholic believes the church doctrine that you cannot know truth on your own, he or she will be reluctant to accept a spiritual vision that goes beyond doctrine. Such people end up feeling that their visions affirm their current beliefs. The more people are attached to their current beliefs, the more they tend to impose those beliefs upon a spiritual vision, either as the vision is occurring or afterwards.

Now add another layer of complexity. Fortunately, the increasing number of visions, especially near-death experiences, has made it easier for people to talk about such experiences.

However, that was not always the case. Even today, many people run the risk that family members or others will not believe their vision. If you have had a vision that has shaken your world view, you tend to need acceptance from others. In describing a vision, people will, almost subconsciously, seek to make it acceptable to the people around them. People might seek to describe and interpret a vision so that it fits within the context of their culture and religion.

On top of that, when a person tries to describe a spiritual vision with words, you have yet another opportunity for the duality of the ego to influence the vision. Words are inherently relative. The same words do not have the same meaning to different people. When a person has a spiritual vision, that person has to some degree managed to reach beyond the relativity of the lower mind. However, when a person attempts to describe the vision, it is inevitable that the description will be influenced by the person's current beliefs.

A person can have a vision in which the person makes contact with a level of the spiritual realm, and therefore it is a valid vision. The exact content or form of the vision can still be affected by the person's consciousness?

That is a good way to describe the central problem concerning spiritual visions. A genuine spiritual vision will show you a glimpse of the spiritual world, but it is extremely important to keep in mind that there is much more to the spiritual world than what you saw. If you walk up to a skyscraper and look through a window on the first floor, can you really say that you know what the entire interior of the building looks like? When you add to this the fact that your consciousness might color the spiritual vision or your interpretation of it, you see the need for great humility. You should never allow yourself to feel that your vision represents a complete and infallible view of the spiritual world. You should never allow your ego to turn it into a weapon that is used against other people and *their* spiritual visions.

I am fully aware that as long as people are trapped in duality, they will always feel threatened when other people have different spiritual visions. They will often allow the pride of the ego to make them feel that their vision and their teaching is more true than anyone else's. The more mature spiritual seekers, the people in the top ten percent, should be able to see through these games played by the ego. They should be able to accept that the true value of a spiritual vision lies in the fact that it demonstrates that there is more to reality than the duality consciousness. You should not allow your ego to use the actual form and content of a vision to reinforce an outer belief system. You should use one vision as a springboard for gaining even better visions that show you a wider view of the spiritual world.

This sounds very complicated, and I can't help but think of the many people who have used the differences between spiritual visions to reject the validity of all spiritual visions or even reject the spiritual side of life. How would you respond to that?

By reminding them of the old saying that you shouldn't throw the baby out with the dirty bath water. If you want to make an honest evaluation, you need to understand the true purpose of spiritual visions:

- The vision demonstrates that there is something beyond your normal level of awareness.

- The vision demonstrates that there is something beyond the material world.

- The vision demonstrates that you can reach beyond your normal level of awareness, reach beyond the material world, and have a direct experience of a higher level of reality.

- The vision demonstrates that there could be a way to look at reality that is beyond your current beliefs and your current belief system.

- The vision demonstrates that the concept of a spiritual path is real. There is more to know, and you can know it by finding the key of knowledge.

When you accept these facts, you should be able to reason that the purpose of a spiritual vision is to encourage you to walk the path. As you do so, you will gradually replace the dualistic beliefs of your ego with a higher understanding that is based on a non-dualistic view of reality. Thereby, you will gradually get a clearer perception and a deeper understanding of God's truth. That is why you see the most spiritual people becoming more and more humble, more and more loving and less and less attached to dualistic beliefs.

The central concept here is that you must never allow a spiritual vision to reinforce the ego's beliefs that it knows everything and that its current knowledge is the absolute truth. Instead, the Conscious You should use a spiritual vision as a proof that it is possible to reach beyond the mental box of the ego. Your current beliefs are not the absolute truth. They are the highest expression of truth that you are able to grasp with your current level of consciousness, yet there could be many levels of understanding beyond what you know right now. Let us look at the situation of an individual lifestream. The Conscious You has built a false sense of identity. This identity is comprised of false ideas and beliefs that are stored at the deepest level of the subconscious mind. The Conscious You has put pieces of colored glass into the kaleidoscope of self. The person now finds the spiritual path and realizes that the purpose of walking the path is to attain a higher understanding of the spiritual reality. As I have said before, a Conscious You cannot exist in a vacuum. If a person abandoned all of its dualistic beliefs, it would lose its foundation. The Conscious You would lose its sense of identity without which it simply cannot cope with the world, and the person might end up in a mental institution. Obviously, I have no desire to see that happen to anyone.

It is extremely important that people see the spiritual path as a gradual climb. In reality, all people are constantly walking the spiritual path even though most are not aware of it. When a person becomes consciously aware of the path, it must begin at its present level of consciousness and then take the very next step. As the Conscious You takes the next step, it achieves a slightly higher understanding that allows it to throw out a few pieces of colored glass without losing its foundation. When the person begins this process, there might be so many pieces of colored glass that the pure light of the spiritual self cannot shine through to the person's conscious awareness. Incidentally, this explains why many people deny the existence of God; their kaleidoscope is so packed with dualistic beliefs that no spiritual light can shine through to the Conscious You.

As the Conscious You continues to remove pieces of colored glass, it will eventually reach a point at which a beam of light can shine through the kaleidoscope to reach the Conscious You. At that moment, the person has a spiritual vision or an intuitive flash. It suddenly sees or understands something that is above and beyond the ego's mental box. However, take note that one beam of light shining through the kaleidoscope does not mean that the kaleidoscope is free from colored glass. Even though the person has had a spiritual vision, it still has many dualistic ideas and beliefs as part of its sense of identity. Those false beliefs can influence the spiritual vision as well as the person's interpretation and description of that vision.

A spiritual vision does not have to be completely pure or objective in order to be valuable. It is not the purpose of a spiritual vision to give a full and complete view of the reality of God. The purpose of the vision is to give a person a direct experience of a state of consciousness that is beyond the dualistic consciousness. The exact form or content of the vision is not nearly as important as the experience itself. One obvious value of a spiritual vision is that the person is greatly encouraged. The person realizes that the spiritual path is real and that it is possible to attain a higher state of consciousness. Spiritual visions have often been a great encouragement to people and have caused them to redouble their efforts to walk the path.

I hear you saying that if we are to avoid having spiritual visions become a source of conflict, people need to accept that an outer teaching or an inner vision is not meant to give you the final, absolute, infallible or unchangeable truth. There could always be a more advanced outer teaching or a higher inner vision?

I agree. The people who belong to the top ten percent – in terms of consciousness, not outer position in society – should be able to realize that you can never allow anything, neither an outer teaching nor an inner vision, to create or reinforce a mental box around your mind. The essence of the spiritual path is to break down all mental boxes until you no longer see reality through a filter of dualistic beliefs. These people should also be able to realize that this is an ongoing process that truly doesn't end as long as you are here on earth. They should be able to let go of the desire to find a teaching that gives absolute truth and the desire to be a member of the only true religion. This is simply a dream that springs from the ego, and you will not progress beyond a certain point until you leave it behind.

Obviously, this will lead people to greater religious tolerance, but I am not saying people need to believe that all spiritual teachings are equally valid or that all visions are true. I earlier talked about the ego creating two relative extremes. One extreme is the belief that there can be only one true religion and thus all others are false. The opposite extreme is the idea that all religious teachings or visions are true or equally valid. This is a dangerous illusion because the duality of the ego can influence any aspect of human affairs. It is quite possible that a spiritual teaching, an organization or a vision can be influenced by the ego. It is important for spiritual seekers to sharpen their ability to discern what is a dualistic illusion and what is a higher understanding. This discernment comes through putting on the mind of Christ, which empowers you to see through dualistic illusions, both inside and outside yourself. You see both the beam in your own eye and the mote in the eye of another.

When you have the mind of Christ, you will not use your discernment to condemn other people. You will never go to the extreme of accusing other people of being of the devil or saying they should be killed in order to purify the earth. You will realize that your current beliefs are the highest truth you can currently grasp and that the same is true for all other people. You never seek to force other people to agree with your beliefs. Instead, you seek to share your beliefs and seek to enlighten people rather than convert them. You do this without force, realizing that it is force that leads to conflict and that the desire to use force always springs from the ego.

You make it sound like there are different levels of spiritual understanding and that the lower levels give a more simplistic explanation that might seem to contradict what is given at higher levels?

That is correct. Think back to my image of teaching math to kindergarten students. When you are trapped in duality, you think that if two spiritual teachings are different, one must be true and the other false. In reality, there is no conflict or contradiction that cannot be resolved through a higher understanding of the issue. Mature spiritual seekers spend their time seeking a higher understanding rather than seeking to defend a limited understanding as an "absolute truth."

Imagine a large observatory with several telescopes. Each telescope shows only a portion of the night sky so you cannot know the totality of the sky by looking through any of the telescopes. You can know the totality of the sky only by stepping outside the observatory and looking at the sky as a whole. If you want to know the totality of God and God's truth, you must be willing to step outside the observatory of religion.

9 | A MYSTICAL APPROACH TO NEW IDEAS

I would like to talk about how people can develop a better approach to religion, and I foresee one topic that can cause some trepidation for a lot of people. You have basically said that we need to stop seeing an outer religious or spiritual teaching as an absolute truth. Instead, we need to develop our ability to experience a higher truth directly inside ourselves. You have also said that we need to avoid seeing a spiritual vision as an absolute truth. I foresee that many people will wonder what to trust? A lot of people have been brought up in a culture that presents a certain belief system as an absolute truth, be it an orthodox religion or science. How can such people let go of their existing belief system and avoid going through a crisis of faith, feeling like they can't believe in anything?

At any given moment, live your life according to the highest truth that you can currently grasp. At the same time, continue to expand your ability to grasp an even higher truth.

Consider the differences between a fear-based and a love-based approach to religion. When you take a fear-based approach, you are always living with the fear of loss. Your beliefs could be wrong, and if one detail is proven wrong, you might lose your faith completely. When you take a love-based approach, you go beyond the all-or-nothing reaction. You see your current beliefs as stepping stones to a higher understanding, and therefore, you could never lose your faith. Instead of walking through life being surrounded by the threat of loss, your life now becomes an exciting journey that leads you toward a deeper and more fulfilling understanding of all aspects of life. Your life becomes a win-win situation.

When you take the love-based approach, you never have to abandon any beliefs. You are always open to the possibility that there is a higher understanding of any issue, and you are actively looking for it by being open to new ideas. Being open does not mean that you see your present beliefs as all wrong or that you have to abandon your present religion. As you grow, you will gradually replace some of your current beliefs with new beliefs. By allowing this process to unfold, you will never actually feel that you have to abandon an existing belief. You simply replace it with a better one.

There is a subtle, but very important, difference between labeling an existing belief as wrong or simply finding a higher understanding that naturally and painlessly replaces the old belief. It is much like a child outgrowing a pair of pants. The child does not blame itself for wearing the wrong size pants or feels that the old pants were bad. The child simply leaves the old pants behind when they no longer fit. Likewise, you should be willing to grow spiritually and as part of the process leave behind beliefs that restrict your mind. You can then adopt a new understanding that allows your mind greater freedom of movement. As Paul said:

> When I was a child, I spake as a child, I understood as a child, I thought as a child: but when I became a man, I put away childish things. (1Corintians 13:11)

I am quite aware that many people have closed their minds to anything that contradicts the Bible. Doing so makes you vulnerable, and some people have eventually come to a point where they could no longer ignore the findings of science. Because they held on to the idea that the Bible had to be an infallible truth, they had to either deny anything that contradicted the Bible or lose all faith in the Bible. Such a reaction represents the black-and-white thinking that springs from the ego. It is your ego and the prince of this world that manipulates you into situations where you feel like you have to make such black-and-white choices. If you are sincere about spiritual growth, you need to become aware of this tendency and avoid letting your ego deceive you into painting yourself into a corner. If you are already trapped, you need to reach for the mind of Christ that will resolve the seeming dilemma.

In this example, the Christ perspective is to say that the Bible does not have to be an infallible or absolute truth in order to be valuable. You can reason that the Bible was given to people who had a much more limited understanding of the material world than people have today. You can accept some of the findings of science – such as the fact that the earth is billions of years old – without losing all faith in the Bible or another religious scripture. Why would the fact that the Bible does not give an accurate description of certain material conditions make it completely worthless? It still has many timeless insights that you can use to enhance your spiritual growth. The key to growth is to realize that people don't have to give up a particular belief system. They have to give up the idea that a particular belief system is an absolute and infallible truth that could never be proven wrong in any detail and could never be expanded. This very idea springs from the separation and duality of the ego and it is completely out of alignment with reality. By giving up this ego-centered idea, you will experience an incredible sense of freedom. You will feel like a huge weight has been lifted from your shoulders. You will feel like an entire world has opened up to you, an exciting world with new discoveries around every corner.

Some people are afraid that if they accept a false idea, they will go to hell.

Once again, a fear-based belief that can only come from the ego. It would be helpful for people to recognize that while you are trapped in the dualistic state of consciousness, you have no chance of recognizing truth in an ultimate sense. People who are spiritually inclined have the ability to recognize ideas that they feel are valid and valuable. The best approach is to follow the ideas that you currently recognize as valid without falling into the trap of believing that these ideas must be absolutely true or even infallible. You should always see your current beliefs as stepping stones to a higher understanding of life. If you will maintain this approach, you will continue to move forward on the spiritual path. As long as you continue to move forward, you are doing what God wants you to do.

It is perfectly true that your ego and the prince of this world are constantly seeking to make you believe in false ideas, and it is prudent to be on guard against this. The biggest threat to your growth is not that you believe in a false idea. The biggest threat is that you keep believing in a false idea because you think it is a true idea and you are not willing to question that belief. It is extremely important for people to understand the truth in the following statement:

> And ye shall know the truth, and the truth shall make you free. (John 8:32)

The ego and the prince of this world are manipulating people through deception, meaning that they don't want you to have the truth. They want to withhold information precisely because they know the truth will make you free from their control. Throughout the ages, you will see that the lowest ten percent of the people have been trying to control the population by withholding information. Many religions have been influenced by this mindset, and a perfect example is the Catholic Church during the Middle Ages.

The absolute truth is that God wants you to have the highest understanding you can currently bear. The people who are in the greatest danger of being controlled by their egos are those who believe in fear-based, dualistic doctrines and who have closed their minds to anything beyond those doctrines. It is true that many open-minded people will come across some incomplete or false ideas. If you are always willing to transcend your present understanding and constantly seek answers from within, you will eventually go beyond such false beliefs. It is the people who are not willing to transcend their current beliefs who end up getting stuck in false beliefs. If you fear the devil, you should realize that he finds it very easy to manipulate people with closed minds whereas it is much more difficult for him to trap people who are constantly expanding their understanding. God has nothing to hide, but the devil has a lot to hide because he is the father of lies. In the light of Christ truth, all lies instantly disappear. Contrary to popular belief, God does not require you to be perfect in the sense that you know everything. Life is an ongoing process, and as long as you are on earth you should assume that you have more to learn. Let go of the idea that in order to be saved you have to believe in ideas that are absolutely true or infallible. In order to be saved, you have to attain a higher state of consciousness. The key to attaining this state of consciousness is that you keep expanding your understanding of life by using the key of knowledge. As long as you keep expanding your understanding and raising your level of awareness, you are on the path to salvation. As long as you keep moving at the greatest speed with which you are capable, you are doing everything that God requires of you. Simply let go of the sense that you have to become perfect in an instant. God does not make such unrealistic demands of its sons and daughters.

As you climb the path, it will be helpful to develop an attitude of not taking anything for gospel. Do not accept that an outer expression of truth is absolute or infallible. Be willing to use every idea as a way to get intuitive insights. Open your mind and heart to an inner experience of truth. Keep the attitude that there might be a higher expression of truth than your current belief system, a higher understanding than what you can grasp with your current level of consciousness. The process of learning will not stop unless you decide that you have found an infallible truth and have nothing more to learn.

You are not saying that people should be open to any and all new ideas, are you?

The Buddha gave the perfect response. He said: "Accept nothing that is unreasonable; discard nothing as unreasonable without proper examination."

How do people conduct a proper examination?

You first of all need to realize that human emotions and the human intellect are relative faculties that cannot give you a proper evaluation of a new idea. For example, many orthodox or fundamentalist religious people are afraid of new ideas, meaning that their emotional bodies become agitated when they are confronted with an idea that goes beyond their present beliefs. Such people literally feel threatened by truth, as demonstrated by the way the fundamentalist people dealt with me 2,000 years ago.

Obviously, this fear-based reaction springs from the ego, and you need to neutralize it. To do this, adopt the attitude that an idea cannot hurt you unless you absorb it and make it part of your identity. You never let an idea into the deeper parts of your mind without proper examination. You might envision that you have a screening room in your mind, and no new idea gets beyond that room until you have examined it and found it valid.

You also need to neutralize the intellect because it can function only by comparing a new idea to your existing beliefs. This often becomes an open invitation whereby your ego can manipulate you into rejecting all ideas that go beyond what it wants you to believe. The intellect can argue for or against any idea without finding a final answer so it is not suited for making important decisions.

Instead of using the emotions and the intellect, use your intuition, use your heart. If the idea rings true in your heart, accept it and change your life accordingly. If the idea does not ring true, simply ignore it. Do not fall into the trap of making a judgment with the outer mind that this must be a false idea or that the person or organization promoting it must be a false teacher. Simply ignore the idea and continue to look for ideas that do ring true. If an idea does not ring true to you, there are two possibilities. The idea might indeed be a false idea and you have developed the discernment to recognize that. The other option is that the idea is so different from, so far beyond, your current beliefs that you are not able or willing to accept it. If that is indeed the case, you do not want to make an outer judgment that the idea is false because that might prevent you from accepting the idea later and thereby taking a major step forward on your path.

Let me assure you that one of the greatest obstacles encountered by seekers on the path is preconceived – and incorrect – ideas about what must be true and what must be false. Almost all human beings have been manipulated by their egos into believing that certain true ideas are false and that certain false ideas are true. For example, many inherently spiritual people accept certain ideas promoted by scientific materialism and thereby ignore their own spiritual natures. Other people have come to accept certain Christian doctrines and refuse to look beyond the teachings of a particular church.

People will inevitably reach a point from which they can make no further progress until they correct a particular false belief. They must accept that an idea, which they have so far believed to be false, is actually true. If people do not realize that they rejected the idea because of a limited state of consciousness, they will not be willing to change their viewpoint. They will literally become stuck at that level of the spiritual path, and they might not progress for the remainder of this lifetime.

Few things burden the heart of a spiritual teacher more than seeing students who are stuck at a certain level of the path because they have rejected a true idea and labeled it as a false idea. For example, some of the people who reject their own spirituality become so disillusioned with life that they sink into depression or even suicide. This is all caused by the fact that, at some point in their past, they labeled a true idea as a false idea and they are not willing to go back and change that decision.

If you are not quite sure about the validity of an idea, simply "put it on the shelf," the shelf located in the screening room in your mind. Decide that as you continue to increase your understanding and raise your consciousness you will, at some point in the future, be able to make a better evaluation of the idea. As you climb the path, you will increase your discernment, and it will become increasingly easy for you to know the difference between true and false ideas. You will no longer need to judge ideas with the outer mind because you will get intuitive insights about the validity of a new idea.

This uncertainty is exactly why some people cling to an outer teaching or doctrine and believe it to be reliable, perhaps even infallible.

Yes, but the need for outer certainty, outer security, springs from the ego. Deep down, the ego knows it is a house built on sand so it can maintain its control over the Conscious You only by offering it security. It does this by seeking to make the Conscious You believe that an outer teaching is the absolute truth and that an outer religion can guarantee your salvation.

When the Conscious You lost contact with the spiritual realm, it felt very vulnerable, and it decided that it didn't really want to make decisions. It created the ego to make decisions for it, and as long as the ego can maintain the illusion that it has everything under control, the Conscious You can feel secure in letting the ego run its life. That is why you see so many people who do not grow spiritually until they experience a major crisis that suddenly awakens the Conscious You and makes it realize it has to take responsibility for itself instead of relying on the ego. I realize that in the beginning it can be frightening for the person to face its own insecurity. If the Conscious You truly understands the spiritual path, it can quickly make contact with its Christ self whereby it will become a house built on rocky ground. I attempted to explain this in my parable about the house built on sand (Matthew 7:26). Your Christ self can be viewed as your internal teacher who can truly give you a higher understanding of any aspect of life through intuitive insights. I talked about the Christ self when I said:

> But the Comforter, which is the Holy Ghost, whom the Father will send in my name, he shall teach you all things, and bring all things to your remembrance, whatsoever I have said unto you. (John 14:26)

There is nothing wrong with using a specific teaching, such as a religion, as a foundation for your spiritual path. There is nothing wrong with using a certain belief system or doctrine as a guiding rod for evaluating new ideas. Nevertheless, I must caution all sincere seekers to avoid letting your guiding rod become a prison for your mind. As you diligently walk the path of personal Christhood, you will naturally find that you have less and less need for an outer guiding rod because you attain the inner guiding rod of direct contact with your Christ self. You will begin to get reliable answers from within instead of having to compare new ideas to an outer doctrine.

As long as we are here on earth, we will not know the fullness of God's truth?

It would be extremely arrogant to assume that a human being could know the totality of God's truth. The best foundation for spiritual growth is to assume there is more to learn. It will be extremely helpful to keep in mind that the truth of God is beyond the limitations, the divisions, the labels, the images, the concepts and the words that you find in the material world.

All true religion was based on a spiritual vision or revelation. The vision formed the open door to a direct experience of truth. The outer description of that vision, expressed in words, is only an approximation of the truth. If you want to know the truth of the vision given to a seer, a prophet or a mystic, you must attain your own vision. You cannot know the truth if you only study the outer description.

As an illustration of this, imagine that you have grown up in a culture in which people are forbidden to look directly at the sun. Such cultures have existed in the past. In such a culture, people never see the sun; they only see reflections of the sun. The sun always remains the same, yet the reflection of the sun can take many different forms. If the sun is reflected by the moon, the reflection is different than when the sun is reflected by the ocean, by a lake, by a flowing stream, by a pane of glass or by a metallic surface.

When you begin to attain Christhood, you realize that all of the reflections came from the same source. They all reflect the same sun, even though the reflections are different. There is only one spiritual truth, but it is a living truth, a truth that is beyond all images and words found in this world. The images and descriptions found in this world are reflections of the Living Truth of God. They are not meant to give you an absolute image of the truth. They are meant to show you that there is something beyond this world.

Imagine that you take a photograph of a river. The photograph is accurate in all respects but one because it does not show that the river is constantly moving. If a person had never seen an actual river, he or she might believe the water is frozen in place. By nature the river is constantly flowing. When you attain Christhood, you do not seek to take a still photo of God's truth, and you do not worship an infallible doctrine. Instead, you joyfully flow with the ever-moving river of God's truth. You go with the wind of the Holy Spirit that bloweth where it listeth (John 3:8).

When you see the reflection of the sun in a shiny surface, you are not meant to worship the reflection or accept that it is all you could know about the sun. Simply dare to lift your gaze and look at the source itself instead of the reflection. Do not confine your quest for truth to the outer expressions of truth. Follow in the footsteps of the prophets who brought you those outer descriptions and seek to attain your own inner experience of God's Living Truth. I promise you that if you will seek with an open mind and heart, you will find that truth (Matthew 7:7). Can you know everything about the sun by studying the moon? If you will knock on the door of direct inner experience, you will have that experience. Dare to reach for the sun and stop worshipping its reflections.

10 | A NONVIOLENT APPROACH TO RELIGION

Based on what you have said so far, it seems to me that people need to develop a less confrontational approach to religion. How would you like people to approach religion and how would you like them to deal with followers of other religions?

I first of all want people to attain an approach to religion that is completely and totally nonviolent. Then I want them to teach – through example – that nonviolent approach to others.

As I have said before, the true goal of spiritual growth is union with a higher part of your being, namely your spiritual self. To attain this union, you must enter the kingdom of God that is within you. This requires that you overcome the idea that you are separated from God by an impenetrable barrier or that anything in this world – including your own ego, a religion, other people or the devil – can stand between you and God. You need to fully accept and absorb the eternal truth that your salvation does not depend on anything outside yourself. It is exclusively a matter between you and God. When you fully internalize this truth, you will not feel threatened by the fact that other people have beliefs that are different from your own. Why would you feel threatened by the beliefs of other people when you realize they cannot keep you out of the kingdom of heaven? When you no longer feel threatened by other people or their beliefs, you have no reason to use force or violence in dealing with other people. You will then have followed my saying:

> If ye love me, keep my commandments. (John 14:15)

Specifically, you will be able to keep my commandments to love your enemies, to resist not evil and to always turn the other cheek. What I was commanding people to do was to leave behind the fear-based reactions that spring from the ego. Only when you do this, can you be completely nonviolent. Only then will you have fulfilled one of my most important commandments:

> For the prince of this world cometh, and hath nothing in me. (John 14:30)

This often misinterpreted statement refers to the fact that when you become completely nonviolent, you no longer feel threatened by anything in this world. The prince of this world, including your own ego, no longer has any "hooks" in your psyche whereby he can manipulate you into a fear-based reaction. Only then will you have attained true spiritual freedom, meaning freedom from duality and separation.

I think this will seem a bit lofty to many people. Can you give us a way to get started on the process?

You can begin by contemplating and absorbing the truth that the earth is a cosmic schoolroom for lifestreams. People learn by making choices, and everything revolves around free will. God has given you free will, and that is why your personal salvation does not depend on anything outside yourself. It depends exclusively on choices you make. I am fully aware that many people give away their power to make choices, allowing their egos, other people or human institutions to make decisions for them. Such people are actually abandoning their responsibility, and it will not free them from reaping the consequences of the choices made by others.

If someone manipulates you into killing people in the name of God, it is no excuse to say: "But they made me do it." They only made you do it because you gave away your power and responsibility to make decisions. In reality, you made the decision to do that, and you are still responsible for the consequences of that choice.

The good news is that God only made you responsible for your own salvation; God did not make you responsible for the salvation of other people. This realization can be a great help in terms of developing a nonviolent approach to religion. The reason being that you do not need to feel that you have to save anyone else—only yourself. If you look at the history of religious conflict, you will see that a major ingredient has always been the belief that "Because we belong to the only true religion, we have to convert everyone else in order to prevent them from burning forever in hell. It is in their own best interest that we convert them, and it is acceptable that we use any means to do so, even force or violence."

You will never be able to enter the kingdom of God within you as long as you feel you have to drag the rest of humanity – or even one person – with you. The reason being that you will believe your salvation depends on something or someone outside yourself. Other people cannot enter the kingdom of God within *you;* they must enter the kingdom of God within themselves.

It will also be a great help to spend some time honestly considering what you want to get out of your involvement with religion. What is it you hope to accomplish through your involvement with religion? As I said, human beings have lost contact with their source and with the reality of God. The purpose of religion is to help them get back to a conscious recognition of who they are as spiritual beings. If you study the lives of the most spiritual people, and you can find them in every religion and even outside the field of religion, you will see a clear pattern. At some point in their lives they all realized that what they really wanted was to come closer to God. Some of them even realized that they wanted to be one with God and that such oneness is the divine birthright of every lifestream. For those who find this a little difficult to accept, you could say that these people wanted to attain union with their spiritual selves, which they saw as God.

If you decide that the result you want to get from your personal involvement with religion is to come closer to God, you have to take a hard look at your outer beliefs, your attitude toward religion and your religious activities. You need to evaluate whether your current approach helps you come closer to God or whether it pulls you in the opposite direction. If you are engaged in a religious activity that promotes an exclusivist, judgmental or dogmatic attitude, claiming that this religion is the only true religion and that unless you believe a certain outer doctrine you will go to hell, then that religious activity is probably pushing you further away from closeness to God. This does not necessarily mean you have to abandon the outer religion, but it does mean you have to find a different approach.

10 | A Nonviolent Approach to Religion

Can we learn anything from the way you and the other spiritual beings in the spiritual realm deal with your differences?

Certainly, and it will help to understand how we of the ascended masters see ourselves. We have a direct experience of the reality of God. We realize that even though we are different, we all came from the same source. Behind our differences, we are all one. The true goal of religion is to make every human being realize that he or she is actually one with the spiritual self and through that spiritual self one with God. When you begin to achieve that oneness on a personal level, you begin to understand that everything is made from God's substance. When you realize this truth, you see that all of the other people running around on this planet are also made from God's substance. They came from the same spiritual source from which you came.

When you come to that realization, you see that all of the divisions that human beings have created are ultimately unreal. They are all based on the illusion of the ego, namely that people are separated from their source. This sense of separation exists only in people's minds, and it can continue to exist only as long as people choose to reinforce it through their attention and energy.

The bottom line is: "Do you want your religious activity to bring you closer to God, or do you want it to push you further away from God?" If you want to come closer to God, you must make sure that every part of your religious activities, including your attitude, the doctrines and dogmas you accept and your outer religious affiliation, supports the goal of coming closer to God. If you become aware that some aspect of your current religious involvement does not bring you closer to God, you need to make a balance sheet. You need to compare the cost and the benefits of continuing that activity.

I am aware that many people gain a sense of security, familiarity and belonging from their involvement with a church, a community or a group. These can be very important advantages, and many people are reluctant to let go of them. However, in the end you need to decide whether you want to cling to this outer sense of security and familiarity, and in the process sacrifice the inner sense of oneness with God, which I can assure you is the ultimate sense of security and the ultimate sense of belonging. That is why I said you have to be willing to lose, meaning leave behind, every aspect of your life in order to win the Christ consciousness (Matthew 16:25).

Should people abandon a church or community if it doesn't bring them closer to God?

I am not saying that you necessarily have to abandon your current religious affiliation. That is truly an individual matter, and it depends on your personal path. You should begin by trying to refine your interaction and approach so that it can serve the purpose of bringing you closer to God while keeping you in your community. If you, after careful consideration, find that your current affiliation or practice cannot be refined so that it brings you closer to God, then you have to make some hard decisions. You need to decide how badly you want to come closer to God.

Remember that in order to follow me, some of my disciples had to leave their nets (Matthew 4:19-20). The nets that my disciples had to leave were not simply the physical nets they used for fishing. This was merely a symbol of their entanglement with the world. To truly follow me into the Christ consciousness, you have to be willing to let go of any and all attachments to the things of this world, including your ego and the consciousness of duality.

I am aware that this will sound scary to many people. I am not saying that you have to let go of the things of this world. I am saying that you have to let go of *your attachments* to the things of this world. There is a very real and very important difference, and if you will meditate on it, you will come to understand that when you are not emotionally attached to something, letting go of it is not a loss. When you are nonattached, you never lose a limited belief; you only gain a wider understanding of life. Why keep yourself in a state of consciousness in which you constantly fear loss? Why not rise to a frame of mind in which life becomes a continual string of mind-expanding discoveries?

It seems to me that some people don't want to come closer to God. I remember feeling that way when I was younger. I didn't want to come closer to an angry God who didn't make sense.

I can relate to that feeling. Contrary to the popular image of Jesus, I had that feeling myself during my teenage years. The image of an angry God presented by the orthodox Jewish religion was repulsive to me. I rejected that God. However, I did not go to the extreme of rejecting all spirituality. Instead, I kept searching for a deeper understanding of God, a better image of God. I did not find that image until I had my own mystical experiences which culminated during my 40 days in the desert.

What I would say to people with this attitude is simply that they might want to consider whether their negative feelings are caused by God, or whether those feelings might be caused by a false image of God with which they have been indoctrinated. A bit of honest soul searching would for most people reveal that it is actually a false image of God that causes their negative feelings toward God. Once you reach that realization, the Conscious You can choose whether it is willing to free itself from the illusion of the false image and make an effort to build an honest, direct, personal relationship with God.

What about people who only want to follow rules and seem to think it is wrong to express individuality, especially in the field of religion?

There are two basic types of people in the world. One type is what I call the creators, namely people who are good at coming up with new ideas and seeing the big picture. The other type are the organizers who are good at handling details and providing stability. These two types of people are actually the expressions of the two basic forces that create the world of form, namely an active, or expansive, force and a contracting, or stabilizing, force. As illustrated in the Taoist symbol of the Tai-Chi, both forces are needed in order to create the universe. Creation occurs only when there is a harmonious interaction between the two forces. As an example, creators are good at coming up with ideas to start a business, but they can rarely run a company. To provide stability and longevity, you need the organizers.

A lifestream is created with both tendencies but one tendency is usually dominant. When the lifestream descends into the lower state of consciousness, it often begins to take the dominant tendency into the extreme whereby it becomes unbalanced. When a creator goes into the extreme, he or she becomes a rebel who refuses to follow any laws or directions. When an organizer goes into the extreme, he or she becomes a judge or a letter-of-the-law person who wants everyone to follow all outer rules to the letter.

10 | A Nonviolent Approach to Religion

Most religions were started by creators who were able to draw down a spiritual vision. You might note that I often broke established rules, as when I healed a man on the sabbath (Mark 2:27). Most religions were later taken over by organizers who insured the longevity of the religion. Unfortunately, when the organizers turn judges, they no longer allow any kind of individuality or creativity to be expressed within the context of what they now see as their religion. They want to create outer rules and doctrines for everything, and they want people to follow the laws to the letter.

To get back to your question, a lifestream was created with a unique individuality. When you decided to venture into the material universe, you were given a basic package for your journey. That package was your God-given individuality and a portion of God's energy. These were your "talents" given to you by your spiritual parents (Matthew 25:14).

God sent you into this world with the command to multiply and take dominion over the earth (Genesis 1:28) This does not mean that people should indiscriminately destroy their environment out of greed. It means that God wants you to multiply your talents and express your individuality in order to create a better world—a world aligned with God's laws. You were designed to express individuality and creativity in all aspects of your life, including your spiritual life. God does not want you to bury your talents; God wants you to multiply them. Doing so is an expression of the highest form of love. The multiplication of your talents is what creates love; it is love in action. One might say that love is to be more than you are, more than you were created to be. Love is self-transcendence, meaning that you are willing to lose your limited sense of life in order to unite with a greater sense of life. You are willing to let your ego die on the cross so that the Conscious You can be resurrected into the Christ consciousness in which you are one with God. If a religion does not allow the expression of creativity and individuality, how can that religion possibly serve to bring God's kingdom to earth? How can that religion be an expression of love that inspires people to enter the kingdom of God within them? It will only serve to maintain status quo by restricting growth, which has been the unfortunate role of all orthodox religions.

The conclusion is that God wants religion to have room for creativity and individuality. However, God wants that creativity and individuality to be expressed in a way that is in harmony with its laws. This is where the creators and the organizers usually clash. The only way to express your God-given individuality and creativity is through the Christ consciousness. When people are trapped by the ego, the creators turn rebels and the organizers turn judges. The rebels refuse to acknowledge any rules, and the judges want everyone to follow rules. The two will inevitably clash.

To fully understand this, it is necessary to reach back to what I said about spiritual cycles. We are now entering an age in which there is a great need for spiritual renewal. We of the ascended masters are releasing spiritual energies to drive that renewal. As a result, you are currently seeing a polarization in the spiritual life of this planet. Some people are running with the new energies, and examples are the New Age movement and the mystical movements within traditional religions. Other people are resisting the change, as you see in many orthodox or fundamentalist movements.

Those who run with the new energies are the creators, but as long as they are trapped in an unbalanced state of consciousness, they will not be able to bring about a true change in the spiritual life of the planet. For example, you see many New Age people who believe that co-creation with God means that you have total freedom to create whatever you want. People do indeed create their own reality, but that does not mean people can do whatever they want with no regard for how it affects others. The essential point here is that you express your creativity in harmony with the laws of God. If you do not, you will harm yourself and the whole, meaning that your creation will self-destruct.

Those who resist change are the organizers, but as long as they are trapped in an unbalanced state of consciousness, they cannot fulfill their proper role. These people understand the importance of being in harmony with God's law, but because they no longer have a direct contact with the spiritual realm, they are not actually seeing God's law. They are attempting to make everyone conform to an outer doctrine and an outer law. They think the outer doctrine or law is infallible so it can never change. They resist change and want everyone else to do the same. In reality, God's law is dynamic and there are also levels of God's law corresponding to different levels of consciousness. That is why the Old Testament presents one level of law, for people in a lower state of consciousness, and the New Testament presents a higher law.

If true spiritual progress is to come about, it can happen only when a critical mass of people attain a certain level of Christhood. Thereby, the organizers and creators will become balanced and they will be able to fulfill their proper roles. The creators will bring forth new ideas, and those ideas will be in harmony with the laws of God. The organizers will provide stability without restricting creativity and individuality. Once again, balance is the key to progress on the path. The Middle Way is always superior to extremism.

When you say that the ego affects the way we see everything, you almost make it sound like every person is creating his or her personal belief system?

That is exactly what I am saying. The ascended masters release spiritual truth, human beings create religion. There are currently seven billion belief systems, or religions, on planet earth. When you are trapped by the ego, you see everything through the filter of duality. As an example, take the Catholic Church which has a well-defined – although contradictory and illogical – outer doctrine. Most Catholics will say that they believe in and accept the official church doctrine. If you go inside people's minds, you will see that each person has an individual understanding or mental image of the outer doctrines. That is why so many Catholics manage to feel they are good Catholics while refusing to follow most of my commandments or the rules of the outer church.

Many Catholics are not consciously aware of how they have created their own image of the Catholic doctrines, and if you ask them to consider it, they will deny the existence of such an image. It is a basic fact of life that you see the world through the filter of your own consciousness. Your religion is not something that exists outside your mind; it is an inner image that exists only in your mind. Obviously, a group of people can have similarities in their inner images but they also have many differences. Most people completely fail to see that their world view is a mental image influenced by their egos and the consciousness of duality. They believe it is the only true or only possible world view, and that is why they feel threatened by opposing views. If you look at history, you will see that some of the greatest atrocities have been committed by people who were not willing to admit that they saw reality through a filter. These people thought that their personal belief system represented an ultimate and infallible truth. It was their duty to force everyone else to conform to their beliefs and to force the entire universe into their mental boxes. It is far better, for yourself and others, to consciously acknowledge the fact that you see the world through the filter of your own consciousness. You cannot solve a problem until you acknowledge the existence of the problem. Once you realize that the contents of your consciousness affect your view of reality, you can begin to do something about it. You can purify the contents of your consciousness and you can learn how to overcome the manipulation of your ego.

The biggest problem on planet earth, the only problem on planet earth, is that people are trapped in the dualistic state of consciousness. Until you recognize that fact, you have little chance of escaping duality and putting on the Christ consciousness. If you do not recognize that you are imprisoned, how can you possibly hope to attain freedom?

Many people are reluctant to acknowledge the fact that your actions cannot be evaluated based on a relative human standard. Your actions can be good according to a human standard but still miss the mark of the Christ standard. This is an uncomfortable fact that many religious people are reluctant to consider. Many people have gotten themselves into a state of consciousness in which they feel that as long as they follow certain outer doctrines and rules, their actions must be acceptable in the eyes of God. They feel that they are so good, righteous, spiritual or even holy that God simply has to accept them. This is the way that seems right unto a human, but the ends thereof are the ways of death (Proverbs 14:12). If you do not acknowledge the existence of a higher state of consciousness, you will continue to create from the lower state of consciousness, and therefore you cannot ascend to the spiritual realm. Instead, you will create a magnet of misqualified energy that binds you to earth.

I have experienced that many people do not want to change their view of God. They might have various

negative feelings toward God, but they don't want to change them because they want to keep God in the little box in which they feel they have their relationship to God under control.

That is a common reaction, especially among people who are unwilling to change. The unwillingness to change is usually a direct consequence of the fact that the Conscious You does not want to take responsibility for itself and its situation. If you do not want to take responsibility for your own path in life, the easiest way to avoid this responsibility is to build a world view in which you are the helpless victim of forces beyond your control. Once you have created such a world view, you do not want to revise it. If you could no longer maintain the illusion that you are a victim, you would have to take responsibility and do something to change your situation.

After a lifestream begins to descend into the consciousness of duality, it keeps moving away from union with God. The lifestream sinks deeper and deeper into accepting a false image of God and harboring negative feelings toward God. When the lifestream reaches the lower levels of consciousness, you have a soul who has an absolute hatred toward God. This is what you see in people who are openly rebelling against God, such as satanists and some materialists. As long as the lifestream feels anger or hatred toward God, it has not truly started the spiritual path. The lifestream either wants to avenge itself upon God, or it wants to control God. You find many such people in the two extremes of scientific materialism, which causes people to deny God, and some form of orthodox religion, which causes people to deny the fact that God does not conform to any earthly doctrine. Obviously, both of these paradigms are based on a false image of God, including the belief that God conforms to human opinions and expectations.

After a lifestream turns around and begins to climb back toward a constructive relationship with God, it often goes through a phase in which its relationship to God is based on guilt, fear and doubt. Many such people are involved with religion because they are afraid of what will happen if they do not go to church. While this is better than allowing your anger to move you further away from God, fear is not a good motivation on the spiritual path.

At a higher level, you see people who have overcome most of their fears and who are now involved with religion out of a sense of obligation or duty. They don't go to church because they fear negative consequences, but they don't go to church because they really want to. They go to church because they somehow feel that they *have to*.

I do not condemn any lifestream. I am not saying this to criticize or condemn anyone for their approach to religion. I am saying it because there is an alternative to the negative feelings or the sense of obligation. If people will make an effort to overcome some of their false beliefs and attitudes, they can quickly move into an entirely new relationship with God and a new approach to spirituality. What I truly desire to see is that people's relationship to God and their involvement with spirituality is based on love. I don't want people to go to church every Sunday out of fear. I don't want them to go to church with a sense of obligation that causes them to engage in a rote ritual that does little to open their hearts to a higher understanding of God. I want people to be involved with spirituality because they love something more than their own egos and the human limitations with which they are comfortable.

Millions of people do not belong to an outer church and never engage in something that would be described as a spiritual or religious activity. These people are constantly seeking for a higher understanding of some aspect of life. These people are driven by a deep love for truth, for knowledge, for understanding. Although such people may not consider themselves to be religious, they are nevertheless walking the spiritual path and they are driven by the highest motivation of all, namely love for something that is greater than the ego.

I also see many religious people who go to church because they love some aspect of their church activity. In that respect, it truly does not matter whether you are a minister performing a service or a parent doing child care. It does not matter to what church you belong. Any activity done with love is a spiritual activity and it can help you move forward on your personal path.

I would love to see people let go of their false beliefs about God and overcome the negative feelings, such as anger, fear or a sense of obligation. I would love to see everyone engage in the path because they love something so much that they simply cannot help themselves. They cannot keep themselves from studying, from praying, going to church, serving in various other capacities or whatever they feel moved to do from within. Whether these activities are considered religious in the traditional sense matters not.

Most people have a tendency to be too caught up in the outer activities. In reality, the outer activity, even the results produced by that activity, are not nearly as important to God as the inner attitudes and feelings with which the activity is performed. What really matters to God is the love in people's hearts. A bishop conducting the service with a sense of duty is far less pleasing to God than the little child lighting a candle with the purest love. This explains why I told people that unless they become as little children, they shall not enter the kingdom of heaven (Matthew 18:3). In the spiritual realm all of our actions are motivated by love. We never do something because we fear the consequences or because we want a reward or recognition. Any service performed with love is its own reward. A service performed with love always receives recognition from God, and that is truly the only recognition that matters.

I do not want anyone to feel bad if they cannot currently perform a service out of love. Love is something that can be cultivated by all, but it will often take time to do so. As you climb the spiritual path and begin to remove your false ideas about God, the true love of your lifestream will begin to shine through to the outer awareness. No matter what state of consciousness you currently have, deep within your being is an unconditional love for your spiritual self and for God. Many people have been wounded so many times that they have hidden their love behind defensive walls in an attempt to avoid being hurt by the forces of this world. A person cannot simply bring out the inner love by being told that God wants them to love. Love cannot be faked or forced.

That is why everything related to spiritual growth must be seen as a gradual path. If you cannot currently approach religion and spirituality with love, do not condemn yourself. If you diligently walk the spiritual path, you will gradually and naturally begin to feel and express more love in all aspects of life. Simply start walking the path to the best of your current ability and allow the path to gradually take you out of all negative emotions until the deepest love of your being begins to flow through your conscious awareness.

Love is one of the basic forces of the universe. The nature of love is to expand and to flow. If love is not currently flowing through you, it is simply because your consciousness contains too many blockages. The blockages are the false beliefs and negative emotions that are obstructing the flow of love. Begin to remove those obstructions and love will naturally start flowing through you.

You might recall that I said: "Greater love has no man than to lay down his life for a friend" (John 15:13). This can be interpreted as giving your physical life to save the life of another. However, it can also mean to give your mortal life, your mortal sense of identity, so that you can be the instrument of God's love and thereby inspire other people to walk the path that leads them home. The highest form of love I can envision for a human being is that a person makes an all-out commitment to walking the spiritual path and overcoming the ego, the duality consciousness. Such a person will become a living example who will inevitably inspire others to join the spiritual path.

All true spiritual teachers teach by example. Unfortunately, the lower consciousness has a tendency to elevate a spiritual teacher to an idol, such as has happened to me over these past 2,000 years. If you look beyond the idolatry, you will see that I came to give people an example of a person who has committed his entire life to spiritual growth and who has done so out of love. I very much need those who will make that same commitment today and be examples of people walking the path. Because of the idolatry built around me, I no longer serve as a good example. I need people to exemplify the path of a true spiritual seeker who is driven by a love for truth, a love for God and a love for all other sons and daughters of God. You might recall that I told my disciples to feed my sheep (John 21:16). How do you feed my sheep? By giving them understanding, by giving them the clear vision of the Christ consciousness but first of all by giving them love.

God has given every human being free will. People have used that free will to become lost in the lower state of consciousness. Because God loves every lifestream, every one of its sons and daughters, God wants every lifestream to return home to oneness with itself. However, God does not want lifestreams to return home because of fear or a sense of obligation. God wants lifestreams to return home because they love God, they love their spiritual selves and they love the kingdom of heaven. I need those who dare to be the example of a person who is driven to come up higher, not out of any human motives, but purely out of love. Love one another as I have loved you (John 15:12) by always encouraging each other to come up higher in consciousness.

In reality, you cannot enter God's kingdom without being "made perfect in love" (1John 4:18). Fear will separate you from God so you must let go of the fear that springs from the consciousness of separation and duality. You must enter into oneness with God, and when you no longer see God as being apart from you, you will be in God's kingdom.

Once people have attained a nonviolent approach to religion, they need to teach that to others. How do you foresee that happening?

The only way to truly teach is through example. You cannot teach nonviolence as a theoretical class in college. You cannot decide with your outer will that you must be nonviolent. Trying to do so will only set up a struggle between your conscious will and your ego. Thereby, you become a house divided against itself (Mark 3:25), and your outer mind most likely won't be able to stand against the onslaught of the ego and the forces of this world.

You must become nonviolent by overcoming the duality of the ego that causes you to feel threatened by other people and their beliefs. If you take a look at the religious life on earth, an honest observer will see that the vast majority of preaching, teaching and evangelizing either springs from or is heavily influenced by the duality of the ego. People are seeking to convert others because their egos feel threatened by the fact that other people have different beliefs. Incidentally, many nonreligious people are driven by the same mechanism to spread their beliefs.

You should always keep the following dynamic in mind. Your ego was born out of an illusion, namely the illusion that you are separated from God. The ego has a survival instinct, and it knows that in order to maintain its existence, it must prevent you from seeing through the illusion of separation. To accomplish this goal, your ego seeks to envelop you in a net of other illusions that spring from duality. The ego's strategy is that you become so entangled with these dualistic illusions that you never get down to seeing the underlying illusion of separation. If you are a religious person, the ego will use religion to make you believe in a set of dualistic illusions. One obvious example is the idea that there is only one true religion and that all other spiritual teachings are dangerous. Just look at how many sincere religious people have spent a lifetime promoting one particular religion and denouncing all other religions. Such people feel they have done God's work, but in reality they have wasted a lifetime on defending dualistic illusions that spring from their own egos.

While some people will be unwilling to admit this, the top ten percent should be able to let go of this entire consciousness of seeking to defend your ego's illusions by trying to make the whole world agree with you. It is simply a futile and utterly pointless way to spend your life. When you do let go of this illusion, your motivation for talking to other people about religion will no longer spring from the self-centered needs of the ego.

As with everything else, teaching a nonviolent approach to religion is a gradual process that will evolve as you rise above the ego and put on the mind of Christ. In the beginning stages, you should focus on the need to never attack other people's beliefs. At this stage, you don't need to state that other people's beliefs are wrong; you simply focus on stating the highest truth that you can see. You don't have to challenge the beliefs of others; you simply have to state the truth as you see it.

You also need to have complete respect for the free will of other people. God has given them a right to believe what they want to believe, and at any given moment they are doing the best they can, given their present level of consciousness. This is also true for you. Your present beliefs are not the absolute truth; they are the highest truth you can grasp with your current level of consciousness.

When you understand this, you see that it is not your job to make another person conform to your beliefs. Your job is to help the other person rise to a higher understanding than he or she has right now. You cannot take the approach that all people need to believe in the same teaching or doctrine. You must look at each person as an individual and then seek to help that person rise to a higher understanding. Some people might be able to grow very quickly while others must take one small step at a time.

As a practical example, say you have grown up in a Christian culture and you come in contact with a Muslim. It is not your primary job to convert the Muslim to Christianity. Your primary job is to help the other person discover the universal spiritual path behind all outer religions—the path of love. If the person sees that you have become more loving by following the inner path, he or she will also want to follow it. Because the person has a Muslim background, the person might want to follow that path through the mystical aspects of Islam, such as Sufism. In that case, you should support the person in doing so without seeking to force Christianity upon him or her. As you begin to attain a higher level of personal Christhood, your approach might change. You will now stop thinking about how to help others attain a higher understanding. Instead, you will begin to simply share your beliefs and insights as you are moved from within. You are no longer deciding what to do with your outer mind, you are simply being who you are.

As a result of this, some people will realize that it is part of their mission to challenge people's closed-minded beliefs. If you look at my life, you will see that I systematically challenged the beliefs of the orthodox people of my time. It was my goal to never leave people the same, meaning that I never wanted to leave someone in the same state of consciousness they had when we met. The crucial insight is that you can do this only when you have risen above a certain level of the ego and let go of all attachments. If you are not free of the ego's tendency to force everything, you will inevitably seek to force other people, and therefore you cannot give them the truth that will make them free (John 8:32).

It is the role of a Christed being to challenge people's mental boxes in order to give people an opportunity to expand their boxes or step outside of them. A Christed being will never conform to people's mental boxes, people's expectations. He or she will naturally challenge people's paradigms, but this will not be motivated by the dualistic needs of the ego. Instead, it will be motivated by the love of God that simply cannot leave people stuck in their dualistic illusions. A Christed being will speak truth even if he or she is rejected by the world. Such a being might even be willing to let people persecute or kill him or her in order to demonstrate that no box in this world, not even the illusion of physical death, can imprison a Christed being. You can demonstrate that there truly are no limitations in this world that can prevent you from attaining union with your God. Nothing in this world can prevent you from entering the kingdom of God within you.

Many Christians have a genuine love for you and feel that in order to be loyal to you, they have to be loyal to a particular Christian church. How would you respond?

If you love me, keep my commandments (John 14:15). As I have attempted to explain, if you look for my inner teachings, you will see that all of my commandments lead you in the same direction, namely toward your personal Christhood. I have no higher desire than to see every lifestream on earth attain the fullness of the Christ consciousness. Anything that comes between you and your attainment of the Christ consciousness is contrary to my desire and my commandments.

While I appreciate loyalty, it is always important that loyalty is directed toward the highest possible goal. In order to be true to my commandments, people need to consider the aim of their loyalty. Are you loyal to *me,* the living Jesus Christ, or are you loyal to a man-made image of me, an idol? Are you loyal to the ascended master I am today, or are you loyal to the physical body that died on a cross 2,000 years ago? Are you loyal to my true, inner teachings or are you loyal to a set of interpretations created over the past 2,000 years? Are you loyal to my love-based commandments or are you loyal to a set of man-made commandments that spring from the fear and separation of the ego? Are you loyal to the true church of Christ, which is an inner church, or are you loyal to an outer organization? Are you loyal to the kingdom of God that is within you or are you loyal to the kingdom of man? Are you loyal to the Prince of Peace or are you loyal to the prince of this world? Are you loyal to the true vision of the Christ mind or are you loyal to the dualistic vision of the ego? I could go on, but those who have ears to hear will get the picture. All Christians need to deeply ponder my statement:

> No servant can serve two masters: for either he will hate the one, and love the other; or else he will hold to the one, and despise the other. Ye cannot serve God and mammon. (Luke 16:13)

The inner meaning is that you cannot be loyal to the things of this world, the consciousness of duality, while at the same time being loyal to Christ and the mind of Christ. In order to be loyal to me, you have to overcome all attachments to the things of this world so that you do not become as the rich man who would not sell his possessions in order to follow me (Matthew 19:20-23). Being loyal to Christ means that you are willing to follow this commandment:

> For whosoever will save his life shall lose it: and whosoever will lose his life for my sake shall find it. (Matthew 16:25)

I am not saying you have to actually lose your life. I am saying that you have to *be willing* to leave behind anything in this world, including your loyalty to a man-made organization or doctrine, in order to attain the mind of Christ. I am actually a very easy master to follow—*as long as you are willing to leave behind everything else!*

What do you think about theologians or scholars who spend a lifetime debating how to interpret particular passages in scripture? Or the many religious people who debate whether this or that interpretation is the only true one?

It all depends on motive. If they debate with a true desire to expand their understanding, the debate can lead to growth. If they debate with an ego-desire to force their viewpoints on others – thinking they already know everything – the debate is futile, meaning that it will not lead to growth. In many cases, two people debate the interpretation of a particular scripture, and they are both motivated by the ego-drive for control.

The reality of such a situation is that both people are unable to look beyond the outer teaching and discover the Spirit of Truth. As a result, they are both arguing for a dualistic interpretation of the scripture. Both are saying: "*My* dualistic interpretation is better than *your* dualistic interpretation, therefore I am one of the chosen ones and you will go to hell!" In reality, both people are out of touch with the truth of God. None of them are chosen because none of them have chosen to rise above the ego. It is amazing to see adult human beings spend a lifetime on such arguments. It is like a person who wants to continue playing in a sandbox, even though he has grown into adulthood. I wish all religious people would get out of the sandbox of the ego and base their approach to religion on the rock of the Christ consciousness.

11 | UNITY WITHOUT SAMENESS

I assume that part of overcoming religious conflict is to foster more unity in the field of religion. However, I also assume you don't envision that one religion will replace all other religions?

Obviously, I don't want to see one religion eradicate all others. How could greater unity come about? The current conditions on planet earth – with so much human conflict and suffering – were not created by God and they are not the result of some kind of accident. Human beings have created the current conditions, and they have done so through the power of their minds. They created these conditions by allowing their minds to dwell upon dualistic images and beliefs. God will not simply remove the current problems on earth, even if people ask God to do so.

God gave human beings free will, and people have used that free will to create the current problems on earth. These problems will disappear only when human beings use their free will to uncreate them and begin to create conditions that do not spring from duality. People must rise above the beliefs that caused them to create a certain imperfection, and then God – or rather, the ascended masters – will step in and multiply their efforts. People must stop burying their talents in the "ground" of the ego and start multiplying them (Matthew 25:23).

The only way change could possibly happen is through a raising of the consciousness of humankind. This higher level of consciousness is not likely to be brought about because every human being on earth suddenly decides to raise his or her consciousness. It is far more likely to be brought about because a relatively small number of people decide to raise their consciousness and therefore become a magnet that pulls everyone else up. This is where the top ten percent enter the story. I applaud all of the spiritually minded people who have understood this basic fact and who have decided to do something to raise their consciousness. The only way to bring about true change on this planet is for a critical mass of people, and I am talking millions of people, to make a fully conscious decision to walk the path toward a higher state of consciousness. I have called that state of consciousness personal Christhood, or Christ consciousness, but other names are equally valid.

There are many people, and fortunately the number is growing every day, who are becoming aware of the need to spiritualize their lives. These people come from many different backgrounds, including traditional religion, science or the New Age movement. I am a spiritual teacher, and I do not put people into boxes or judge them according to a relative standard. I love everyone with an unconditional love, and I seek to help and inspire everyone to come up higher. I applaud all those who are making sincere efforts to raise their own consciousness and the consciousness of humankind. No single person is more important than any other single person because "God is no respecter of persons" (Acts 10:34). Consequently, no organization is more important than any other organization. When you look at the current situation on planet earth, I think it should be obvious that there is indeed much opposition to spiritual growth. I know that many people are reluctant to consider the existence of dark forces. Let us simply perform a little thought experiment and imagine that there is a force that is trying to prevent humankind from reaching a new level of spiritual awareness. If such a force did exist, what would be its primary method for sabotaging the efforts of the people who are sincerely working to bring about positive change?

The greatest enemy of spiritual unity is the divide-and-conquer strategy. There are many individuals and organizations who are making a sincere effort to bring a new understanding and a higher level of consciousness. Despite what some of the leaders and members of such organizations claim or believe, there is no single organization that can do this by itself. If a large-scale spiritual awakening is to happen, it can only happen if a large number of people and organizations decide to work together on a common goal.

Here in the spiritual realm there is a great number of spiritual beings who are seeking to inspire humankind. Despite the fact that we are all individuals, we are all working together as part of the same team. We all see the essential unity behind our individuality because we realize that we all came from the same source. Spiritual renewal can be brought to this planet only when millions of people recognize that despite their individual differences, despite their various backgrounds beliefs and belief systems, they are all part of the one Body of God on earth.

The main factor that works against the formation of the one Body of God on earth is the divide-and-conquer strategy. Dark forces and people's egos cannot work against people's free will. They will try to manipulate people into making wrong choices, but people must make the choice to accept dualistic ideas. What makes people vulnerable to this manipulation is that they identify with their egos. Thereby, a lifestream becomes a house divided against itself (Matthew 12:25). People are so divided in their own psyches, divided by their egos, that they are easily conquered by outside forces that seek to pull them into religious conflict.

There are especially two tendencies that make people vulnerable to the divide-and-conquer strategy. One is the ego's need to feel that it is somehow better or above others. Many sincere individuals still have a subtle feeling that they want to be the avant garde who saves humanity. Others have a need to feel that their organization or their efforts are more effective or more important than those of other people. Many individuals and organizations tend to set themselves apart from others and they do not acknowledge the need for cooperation. They feel that they are single-handedly doing God's work and saving the planet, and they want to keep it that way by not recognizing any "competing" organizations. The basis for this is pride, which springs from fear.

Another factor is that some people have a tendency to believe that the only way to save the planet is through one particular belief system or one particular organization. They are not working to raise the consciousness of humankind. Their main goal is to promote one particular belief system, one particular organization or one particular guru as the only way to save the planet. As we have already discussed, there is more than one true religion. In the spiritual realm there is no competition. There should be no competition among those on earth who see themselves as the servants of God. The basis for all competition is fear and pride, which spring from the ego.

I am not making these remarks to criticize or find fault with any particular organization or individual. The only way to create major change on this planet is for people to come together and join forces as the one Body of God on earth. During the

Piscean age people often attempted to force unity by seeking to make their particular organization into the dominant organization. Sometimes they would try to convert everyone else or kill those who would not be converted. In the Aquarian age the belief in one superior organization or belief system is completely and utterly outdated.

I am not advocating that all people join one particular organization or belief system. Instead, I am encouraging people to form a network of individuals and organizations who are willing to work together on the essential goal of raising the consciousness of humankind. Those who have reached a certain level of spiritual maturity, a certain level of personal Christhood, should be able to look beyond divisions and establish a new type of unity, a unity that does not eradicate differences but empowers people to look beyond differences.

In the spiritual realm we are still individuals. We never lost our individuality by letting go of the duality and the divisions of the ego. On the contrary, we won our true God-given individuality. That is what I desire to see on earth, a true unity so that human beings in embodiment do not only form a unity with each other but also a unity with the ascended masters. Thereby, people in embodiment and we, who are the spiritual teachers of humankind, can form a unity and be as Above so below. In the early days of the Christian movement, my disciples were divided over the issue of whether to preach my word to the gentiles. The controversy was resolved by the descent of the Holy Spirit at Pentecost:

> And when the day of Pentecost was fully come, they were all with one accord in one place. (Acts 2:1).

Why did the Holy Spirit descend on that occasion? Because the disciples were of "one accord." This did not mean that they had lost their individuality or differences. It meant that they were united in a sincere desire to know and do God's will instead of the will of the ego. They were united by the higher vision of the Christ mind, a vision that was beyond the duality of their egos. The scriptures also record that I made a promise:

> For where two or three are gathered together in my name, there am I in the midst of them. (Matthew 18:20)

This does not simply mean that whenever people get together and repeat my name, they automatically summon my Presence. In order to do that, they must be willing to reach beyond the divisions of their egos and be of one accord. My name in synonymous with the Christ consciousness, and unless you are willing to reach beyond duality, I cannot fully respond to your call. What I desire to see happen on this planet is that all truly spiritual people will see the need to reach beyond outer differences and divisions. I hope people will come together and be of one accord in a desire to bring forth a higher state of consciousness. If that were to happen, I can assure you that the ascended masters would pour out such a measure of the Holy Spirit that there would not be room enough to receive it (Malachi 3:10). Only the true Holy Spirit can bring true unity among spiritual people.

People need to look beyond the fact that they belong to different religions, have different teachings and even different spiritual visions. They need to look beyond the outer differences that divide them and look for a higher vision that unites them in a common purpose?

Yes, but again, we are talking about a gradual process, and at the beginning stages, many spiritual people will find it difficult to fully let go of the duality consciousness. All truly spiritual people should be able to accept the concept that their true adversaries are not the members of other spiritual organizations. If you see yourself as a spiritual person, you need to see yourself as part of a universal movement that seeks to raise the consciousness of humankind to a higher, more spiritual, level. You need to realize that any other organization that is working to increase people's spiritual awareness is working for the same cause for which you are working. The members of other spiritual organizations are not your adversaries.

If you still need an adversary, you can see it as the force that is working against the spiritualization of people's consciousness. Again, I would hope spiritual people can avoid labeling other people as their enemies and focus on combating ideas. There are indeed many ideas in this world that are promoting an anti-spiritual approach to life. There is ample basis for spiritual people joining forces to combat anti-spiritual ideas.

I also hope all spiritual people will work on refining their discernment. For example, some religious people see science as an enemy of religion, yet is that necessarily the case? Would it not be more constructive to say that the real opposition to spiritual growth comes from the mindset that causes people to close their minds to new ideas. This mindset can be found in both science and religion, as well as in any other field of human endeavor. The real opposition to growth is a mindset, namely the fear-based approach to religion. The real cause of spiritual people is to promote a better mindset, a love-based approach to spirituality. As I said before, this new mindset can be taught only through example.

As people grow in Christ consciousness, they should eventually overcome the need for an adversary and begin to work for God's cause instead of working against the devil. On an individual level, this puts the lifestream back in touch with its original purpose for coming to earth. As I mentioned before, each lifestream was created with a unique individuality, and this gives it the potential to bring a unique gift to this world. The lifestream originally came to earth to bring this gift and thereby help co-create God's kingdom on this planet. The lifestream did not come here to fall into the duality consciousness and then struggle to get back up. The lifestream came with a constructive purpose of expressing its god-given individuality.

As the lifestream grows toward Christ consciousness, it will begin to remember its original purpose and it will uncover its unique individuality. This will give the lifestream an entirely different outlook on life. The lifestream will naturally lose its attachments to the petty human power struggles, and it will come to see them as utterly pointless compared to the grander vision and purpose of its spiritual self.

The lifestream will also begin to see that its higher purpose is not the gratification of the ego. It will then begin to realize that so many people spend their entire lives defending and elevating their egos. The enlightened lifestream will come to see this as an utterly pointless way to spend your life. Instead, the lifestream will want to engage in a higher purpose, a greater cause. That purpose is to help bring God's kingdom to earth through its individual gift and creativity. This mission is not self-centered, it is not centered around the lifestream itself. The mature lifestream realizes that it is part of the whole, namely the Body of God on earth. Its individual mission is like a facet in a large diamond. The lifestream will naturally begin to work for a cause that not only helps itself grow but also helps the entire human race grow.

One might say that a spiritually mature lifestream sees no barriers or contradictions between its own creative expression and the greater cause of God. The lifestream naturally finds the greatest fulfillment in improving the whole, meaning that it begins to find joy in helping others. This will naturally break down the barriers between the lifestream and other people, and the lifestream has overcome the ego-divisions that separate it from other people. The lifestream has truly realized that because it is part of the whole, what is done to the whole is also done to the lifestream. The lifestream will realize that "Inasmuch as ye have done it unto one of the least of these my brethren, ye have done it unto me" (Matthew 25:40).

The lifestream will work for the enhancement of the whole, and in doing so it will find its greatest personal growth and fulfillment. The lifestream will realize that when you multiply your talents to help others, your spiritual self will truly reward you by multiplying your creative powers. You will then enter a positive spiral that leads you directly into the kingdom of heaven, while you are pulling humankind up with you. I can assure you that the joy of feeling one with the whole and feeling one with God is a greater joy than can be imagined by those who are still trapped in the consciousness of separation. While the human ego and the prince of this world might offer your lifestream all of the kingdoms of this world (Matthew 4:8), their offering is like nothing compared to the true gifts of the Spirit. Truly, nothing in this world can compare to the glory you will experience when you give up the ego and immerse yourself in the whole from which you came. At that point, you will feel the glory that I experienced and it will be as true of you as it was of me:

> 1 These words spake Jesus, and lifted up his eyes to
> heaven, and said, Father, the hour is come; glorify thy

Son, that thy Son also may glorify thee:
2 As thou hast given him power over all flesh, that he should give eternal life to as many as thou hast given him.
3 And this is life eternal, that they might know thee the only true God, and Jesus Christ, whom thou hast sent.
4 I have glorified thee on the earth: I have finished the work which thou gavest me to do.
5 And now, O Father, glorify thou me with thine own self with the glory which I had with thee before the world was. (John, Chapter 17)

Some Christians seem to think I am an egomaniac who wants to be worshiped and elevated above all people. My only true desire is to be one with you as you become one with the whole. I desire to see all of my brothers and sisters follow in my footsteps and achieve the oneness that makes them glorified in the eyes of God. When you experience the glory of oneness with God, your only desire is to see all life experience the same glory. When you know that what is done to others is also done to you, you will want only the best for all life.

We cannot create unity among religions unless we go beyond the dualistic state of consciousness?

That is right. True unity among spiritual people cannot be a horizontal unity, meaning that it is based on the consciousness of duality. It must be a vertical unity, meaning that it is based on the Christ consciousness, or whatever you want to call it. When you begin to attain some degree of union with your personal Christ self, you will see yourself as part of a larger whole. You will also see other people as part of that larger whole, and when you bring together a group of people who all have some degree of vertical union with their Christ selves, a spontaneous union will form among them. They will be of one accord through the intermediary of their individual Christ selves; they will be united in spirit.

When the members of various religions attain this individual union with their Christ selves, they will begin to see themselves as part of the Body of God. As the next step, they will begin to realize that they *are* the Body of God on earth while the ascended masters are the Body of God in heaven. People will then realize that, through the Christ consciousness, you become part of the ascended masters, you become our hands and voices on earth. This will lead to the realization that all true religion was given by the ascended masters. Behind the outer differences and dualistic doctrines, there is a deeper unity among the world's religions. All true religions came from the same source and have the same purpose, which is to raise the consciousness of humankind above duality so the kingdom of God can be manifest on earth.

When you break through to this realization, you see that all religious conflict is utterly futile. It has no reality in God and can only spring from the ego and the prince of this world. This can give rise to a true unity among different religions, namely a vertical unity that springs from the Spirit. This unity will recognize that different religions were given to people in different states of consciousness. Each religion is designed to help people rise above a particular aspect of the duality consciousness. The mystical aspect of each religion has the potential to take a lifestream all the way to the Christ consciousness. Each religion – in its original, mystical form – is a worthy and valuable way to freedom from duality. It is this realization, and this realization only, that will replace religious conflict.

12 | RELIGION AND SCIENCE

I would like to touch on the topic of religion and science. I sense that a lot of the people in the top ten percent have been disappointed by orthodox religion, and as a result many of them have accepted a materialistic belief system that rejects all religion. I think it would be helpful if you could comment on how to reconcile spiritual beliefs with science. I would like to begin with your earlier statements that religion is meant to be a description of God, and it should never be allowed to prevent people from striving for a direct experience of God. You do want people to strive for a direct experience?

That is exactly what I want. Imagine a parent who confines his child to a room with no windows. The parent often reads from a book that gives a detailed description of the sun, but the parent never allows the child to go outside and see the sun for itself. Obviously, most people would think that such a parent is strange. Why do they think their heavenly parents would want them to settle for a description instead of experiencing the real thing? The simple fact is that God wants all lifestreams to experience the fullness of its Being. How else can you know that God exists? You cannot prove the existence of God through a material instrument; you can prove it only through a direct inner experience. The mind of Christ is the only "instrument" that can detect the Presence of God:

> All things are delivered unto me of my Father: and no man knoweth the Son, but the Father; neither knoweth any man the Father, save the Son, and he to whomsoever the Son will reveal him. (Matthew 11:27)

As I have now explained many times, the "Son" is the Christ consciousness, and only when you personally attain it can you know God.

When you say that the existence of God can be proven only through a direct inner experience, I can hear many scientists say that a personal experience does not constitute an objective proof.

I would simply ask them to provide me with an objective proof of anything. Just give me an objective proof of anything whatsoever. Show me any scientific observation that is not affected by the mind of the scientist. Scientists have for far too long danced around the golden calf represented by the belief that science provides objective proof whereas religion is entirely subjective. This is simply a dualistic illusion.

We have already talked about the fact that quantum physics has proven that whenever a scientist conducts an experiment, the outcome of the experiment is influenced by the consciousness of the scientist. This has been proven beyond a reasonable doubt, but most scientists have not fully accepted the philosophical conclusion, namely that science is no more objective than any other human endeavor. If scientists fully accepted the discoveries of quantum physics, they would have to admit that it is not possible for a human being to make an observation which is not influenced by the person's consciousness.

We can even apply simple logic. When the scientist is making an observation where is that observation made? It is made in the consciousness of the scientist! A scientist might look through a telescope and think he or she is observing a distant galaxy. However, what the scientist sees through the telescope is light waves. The telescope is not projecting the image of a galaxy. The telescope is simply passing on an arrangement of light waves. It is the scientist who imposes a mental image upon the light waves, calls it a galaxy and then attaches some abstract meaning to the word galaxy.

Your physical senses and all scientific instruments are mechanical devices. They do not show you an image; they only show you light rays (or another form of vibration). It is your mind that conceptualizes an image and projects that image, and the meaning you attach to it, unto the light rays. Incidentally, this proves that you are more than the brain because a mechanical instrument, such as the brain or a computer, cannot conceptualize or ask questions. Only a self-aware being has that ability, and although it happens through the machinery of the brain, the brain is not producing the process—it is simply facilitating it. As near-death and spiritual experiences prove to any open-minded person, the Conscious You can exist independently of the brain.

When a scientist observes an atom, he or she is observing a phenomenon. The phenomenon was not created by the mind of the scientist, and one might say that it has an existence which is independent of the consciousness of the scientist.

However, the phenomenon itself is not an atom. The scientist creates the concept of an atom and imposes it upon the phenomenon. The scientist has not proven the objective, independent existence of an atom. The scientist has proven that there is a phenomenon, but it is not proven that the scientist's conceptualization of the phenomenon is infallible, complete or the only possible one.

The idea that science is automatically objective is inherently flawed. The term "objectivity" normally means something that is not influenced by biases or personal prejudices, the very characteristics of the ego and the duality consciousness. Science is no more objective than the consciousness of the scientist. As long as they are blinded by the duality of the ego – and think everything they see is reality – everything human beings perceive is influenced by their state of consciousness. This is the same for scientists and religious people alike. There is no way for an unawakened human being – meaning a person blinded by duality – to observe anything without observing it through the filter of his or her consciousness.

This does not mean that human beings cannot make accurate and valid observations of the world in which they live. However, such observations can only come about when people begin to understand how consciousness works and how it influences their perception. The theory of relativity clearly states that you cannot make an accurate observation unless you know how your frame of reference influences your observation. Most scientists ignore the philosophical consequences of this theory, and that is why they are unwilling to reach the necessary conclusion, namely that the consciousness of the scientist is always part of his or her frame of reference.

What really needs to happen is that people come to understand how the duality of the ego can make all observations relative. Then they need to reach for the Christ consciousness, which can give them observations that are not colored by the dualistic consciousness of their own egos. True scientific and spiritual objectivity is possible only when a person rises above the duality consciousness and makes an observation from the Christ mind. Science simply cannot attain true objectivity by ignoring consciousness; it can do so only by *understanding* consciousness.

I can already hear the objections that scientists will raise about this. They will completely refuse to accept that science is not objective. Many scientists are as attached to this idea as religious people are attached to the belief that their religion is infallible. If everything we observe is subjective, how can we ever make accurate observations of anything?

The all-important distinction is whether you observe something from the consciousness of duality or from the Christ consciousness. The essence of the ego is that it is relative. When you observe something through the filter of that lower state of consciousness, you can never make an accurate or valid observation or make a valid conclusion. The essence of the Christ consciousness is that it is above the duality of the ego. The Christ consciousness allows you to make truly unbiased observations of the world.

When it comes to observing the world, the physical senses have some obvious limitations. Scientific instruments are a great way to extend the physical senses and allow scientists to observe deeper levels of the material universe. However, there is a fundamental difference between observing reality and interpreting that observation. As I said earlier, what you see is light rays and they have no meaning in themselves. They only attain meaning, and they only become useful, when you put them in a context, meaning that you fit them into your existing world view. However, if your world view is dominated by the duality and relativity of the human ego, it will by definition be inaccurate and incomplete. One might say that even if a scientist made an accurate observation, that in itself would not ensure an objective interpretation and conclusion.

How does your teaching about the Conscious You fit into this?

The key to rising to a higher level of perception is to understand the teaching that the core of your being is a pure self, the Conscious You. This being is self-awareness in its purest form. I realize this will sound like just a theory to people who have not experienced awareness in its purest form, but more and more people are having this experience of pure awareness. Albert Einstein described this experience many times and referred to it as "the mysterious."

Most people are completely identified with what I have called your soul vehicle. This is, as I explain in more detail in the previous books, made up of four levels, namely the identity level, the mental level, the emotional level and the physical level. These four levels of the mind form four filters that color the way you look at everything. Most people perceive the world through the filter of the four levels of the mind, meaning that the physical mind is what is for them the conscious mind. Even though the Conscious You is looking at the world through these filters, the Conscious You does not *become* the soul. The Conscious You is still pure awareness and that means it still has the ability to step outside its perception filter and perceive the world and its spiritual self without any filter. This is what people have traditionally called a mystical experience, but it is actually a natural experience that should be studied by science. It is a life-changing experience to see the world without a filter. As we have talked about with spiritual visions, once you snap back to your normal sense of self, you might begin to interpret the experience through the filter of your soul vehicle. It takes a long process for people to rise to the level where they can learn to systematically step outside their perception filters and where they have purified their filters so much that they can avoid imposing a biased observation on what they see. This is what I call the Christ consciousness.

If scientists would make an effort to reach for the Christ consciousness, they could create a far more advanced world view than what they currently have. With such a foundation, their observations would not only be more accurate, they would also be far more useful. Think about the fact that the ancient Greeks described the existence of atoms. It took centuries before scientists had achieved sufficient knowledge to make practical use of atoms. I can assure you that scientists have already discovered many phenomena that have the potential to create far more advanced – and safer – sources of energy than splitting the atom. Because scientists have an incomplete world view, they do not understand how to make practical use of these discoveries. If scientists would make an effort to attain Christ consciousness, and adjust their world view accordingly, you would see the emergence of more advanced technologies than even the best science-fiction writers can imagine. Again, the basic dynamic is that the ego wants reality to conform to its mental images. A person with some degree of Christ consciousness wants truth rather than the confirmation of his or her existing beliefs.

I think many scientists will claim that if two scientists follow the same procedure and make the same observation, it proves the objectivity of science. The

consciousness of the scientist does not alter the observation.

I agree with you, and I have seen scientists do this many times. However, the fact that two or two hundred scientists follow the same procedure and make the same observation does not prove objectivity. If every scientist in the world put on yellow glasses, they would all make the observation that the sky is green. All human beings have been born with colored contact lenses and most have never seen the world without the lenses, meaning they have no frame of reference for even knowing that their perception is flawed.

During the Middle Ages, millions of people made observations and came to the conclusion that the earth was flat. Nevertheless, the earth was still round. Even if every human being on earth accepts a false idea, the idea does not become true. If two scientists use the same procedure, they might make the same observation. However, the important point is not the observation but the interpretation of it. That interpretation will inevitably be influenced by the consciousness of the scientists.

You might say that two scientists can have different outer beliefs and still make the same observation and agree on the interpretation. If both scientists are trapped in the duality of the ego, their interpretation will inevitably be influenced by the relativity of that lower mind. Every human being is somewhat influenced by the ego. Most people agree on certain ideas or beliefs that spring from the lower mind. For example, many people believe the Bible is infallible whereas others believe scientific materialism is the only true religion. This does not make such ideas correct. Agreement, even widespread agreement, is not the same as objectivity, and this is what most scientists fail to acknowledge. They also fail to acknowledge that all scientists, during their education and upbringing, are subjected to a certain form of mental programming. Scientists can see this so easily in people who grow up in a specific religious culture, yet they often fail to see the beam in their own eyes. The minds of all people have been programmed to accept certain ideas without question. Before Albert Einstein, most scientists had been programmed to believe that matter and energy were two fundamentally different elements, and hardly anyone questioned this idea. Einstein did not submit to this programming and was willing to ask the questions that no other scientist would consider. Some people call the ability to question the unquestionable for genius. I call it a natural effect of Christ consciousness.

I am not saying that there is anything wrong with striving for scientific objectivity. This drive developed as a reaction against the superstition of the Middle Ages, especially the superstition and superficiality of certain church doctrines. The drive for objectivity has been a major factor in bringing humanity into a more rational state of consciousness. I am, however, saying that true objectivity cannot be attained through materialistic means because such means cannot reach beyond the material universe. The claim that there is nothing beyond the material universe is not an objective observation. It is as incomplete as the idea that the earth is flat. One day, when a critical mass of people attain a higher degree of Christ consciousness, this idea will be considered just as primitive as the "infallible" church doctrines it claims to replace.

As long as scientists are influenced by the duality of the ego, even the most sophisticated scientific methods cannot ensure objectivity. I am not thereby saying that such methods are worthless. Scientific methods have indeed enabled people to achieve a higher level of rational knowledge than religious superstition could ever produce. I am merely pointing out that true objectivity can only be attained by rising above the duality of the ego. If a critical mass of people will strive for Christ consciousness, then both science and religion can begin to fulfill their proper roles.

Do you mean that we should also strive to obtain objectivity in the field of religion?

Of course! True spirituality is based on a mystical experience. When you attain a true mystical experience, you rise above the duality of the ego, even if it is only for a moment. Such an experience can indeed give you an unbiased – although not absolute – vision of reality. What has traditionally been lacking in the field of religion is the scientific demand for repeated experiments. The fact that one person has a mystical experience does not necessarily produce a valid or useful vision. What needs to happen is that people use some of the tools developed by science to investigate mystical experiences. This will make it possible for a great number of people to compare their mystical experiences and thereby achieve a far more useful understanding of the spiritual realm.

Take note that there is a difference between having a mystical experience and describing that experience. When you describe a mystical experience, you must relate it to your current world view. If you are not willing to expand your world view, you will distort or limit the experience. If you *are* willing to expand your world view, that adjustment will open up for new experiences and discoveries that will help you expand your world view even more. The image of an ongoing path toward higher understanding should be seen as essential for both scientific and spiritual exploration.

Obviously, a scientific investigation of mystical experiences will require a paradigm shift. Religion must be seen as a systematic way to produce mystical experiences and to give such experiences to a large number of people. Incidentally, this is what the ascended masters have always wanted to see for religion. I never wanted people to turn my mystical experiences into doctrines that prevent them from having the same experience. I wanted all of my brothers and sisters to experience the reality of God.

If I was the only one experiencing God, I might be hallucinating. If a great number of people have similar experiences, we begin to build a body of evidence. This evidence is not an objective proof, but it is an indication that there is something beyond the duality consciousness. The scientific method is based on repeated experiments that gradually build a body of evidence. By applying scientific methods to mystical experiences, people can expand their understanding of the spiritual side of life.

You talked about spiritual cycles and that we are entering a new spiritual age. What would you like to see happen to science in this new age?

A major role of science in the Age of Pisces was to free people from many of the limitations of the material world. When I walked the earth, most people spent all of their time and energy on mere survival. During the past 2,000 years, technological progress has allowed a large number of people to gain free time and energy. Unfortunately, most people are not using their free time according to the original purpose. Because of the split between science and religion, many people have fallen victims to a materialistic state of consciousness. In this state of consciousness people think their lives have no higher purpose, and they spend their free time in a meaningless pursuit of pleasure and entertainment.

The ascended masters gave humankind the gift of science and technology in the hope that when people attained free time, they would use it to pursue spiritual growth. Indeed, millions of people in the Western world have used their free time to focus their attention on the spiritual side of life, whether it be through religion, spirituality or the self-help movement. Unfortunately, millions more have not yet realized the incredible opportunity they have been given by having free time.

The true purpose of giving people free time is to give them the opportunity to direct their attention away from the mechanics of making a living and focus on spiritual growth. You cannot serve two masters. You cannot serve God, meaning spiritual growth, and mammon, meaning the pursuit of pleasure and entertainment. The call to "choose you this day whom ye will serve" (Joshua 24:15) is as relevant today as it was thousands of years ago.

What about the fact that science has helped people overcome many superstitious beliefs about the world, including some beliefs that were so-called infallible religious doctrines?

One of the important functions of science is to give people a clear understanding of the natural laws that God used to create the material universe. In that respect, science has a very important function, but it is also meant to give people the practical tools to improve life on this planet. Over the past few centuries, science has had an important function in terms of helping people overcome some religious doctrines that were clearly superstitious and erroneous. This has helped many people rise to a more rational state of consciousness. I do not want to discount this because it truly has been of great value. Nevertheless, if religion had not been perverted by a dogmatic approach, science would not have had to play this role. If religion, especially the Christian religion, had not gone astray from my original intention, there never would have been a conflict between science and religion. Instead, science and religion would have been seen as two sides of the same coin. Science and religion are simply tools for increasing people's understanding of life. Religion should be a tool for increasing people's understanding of the spiritual side of life. Science should be a tool for increasing people's understanding of the material side of life. The purpose of both tools should be to work together and help people improve the condition of life on this planet, ultimately bringing God's kingdom to earth. God's kingdom includes the abundant life, which means both material and spiritual abundance.

I think neither science nor religion has fulfilled its potential for helping us gain a higher understanding. Both have a tendency to become dogmatic and claim that their current paradigms or dogmas represent the ultimate understanding. How could that be changed?

Once again, let me say that the main problem with the ego is that it tends to impose an image upon reality and then seeks to make reality conform to that image. [For additional teachings on the ego, see three previous books in this series.] You can see that tendency at work in the fields of both science and religion, although I frankly admit that it is more rampant in religious than in scientific circles. Nevertheless, many scientists are attached to the materialistic paradigm and are doing everything they can to force scientific discoveries to conform to that paradigm. Despite the fact that scientific discoveries are clearly pointing to the incompleteness of scientific materialism, many scientists refuse to accept the evidence. One way to change the situation is that people realize how their current state of consciousness and understanding affects the way they look at life. I already mentioned that the theory of relativity states that all observations are relative to your frame of reference. Any person living in a scientific and rational age, even a religious person, should always be on guard and seek to evaluate how his or her current beliefs are affecting all observations and conclusions.

Consider how a caveman would look at the world. These people found themselves in a frightening situation. They were constantly threatened by forces they could not understand or explain. One might say that since then people have been engaged in a process of developing tools for understanding and explaining the world in which they live. Both religion and science are meant to serve as such tools.

It is essential for people to realize that the tools they use to investigate the world will influence the observations they make. As said before, if you put on yellow glasses, the sky will appear green. Unless you realize that you are wearing colored glasses, you might think that what you see through the glasses is reality. When people are seeking to increase their understanding of the world, the basic tool for attaining a higher understanding is to ask questions. A religious seeker or scientist is simply asking questions and then seeking answers.

What is the basis for asking questions? You cannot ask a question unless you have some knowledge about the topic. You must have a foundation for formulating a question. If you know absolutely nothing, like the caveman, you cannot formulate an intelligent question nor can you receive a useful answer. This fact is the basis for the old saying: "The more I know, the more I realize that I don't know." The reason being that when you know more, you can formulate more detailed, questions.

If you tie this to the concept that there are no absolute doctrines, you discover an extremely important principle.

12 | Religion and Science

Humankind's current knowledge in the fields of both science and religion cannot provide an ultimate understanding of the universe. People's current knowledge is simply a foundation that allows them to ask more detailed and more intelligent questions. The essential realization here is that your current knowledge and your current beliefs will limit the kind of questions you are able to formulate. So far, this has nothing to do with the ego. It is simply a basic fact that your current knowledge will limit the kind of questions you can imagine. Before scientists had discovered subatomic particles, how could they formulate questions about the behavior of such particles?

When scientists have gathered data, they seek to fit it into existing theories. The existing theories form the basis for scientific exploration. If scientists discover data that cannot fit into existing theories, they should seek to adjust their theories to fit the data. If they refuse to do so – for example by clinging to the materialistic paradigm – they will put the evolution of science on hold. Incidentally, any religion should be viewed the same way, namely as a temporary platform for attaining a deeper understanding of the spiritual side of life.

Both science and religion are tools for investigating the world. They can be seen as languages that allow people to formulate questions and put the answers into a larger context, namely their world view. The problem in the fields of both science and religion is that most people fail to recognize how their current knowledge and beliefs influence the kind of questions they are able to ask and therefore the answers they are able to obtain. People often become attached to a certain approach to life, and they want to believe that it gives them an ultimate and accurate understanding of reality.

Few people are open to the realization that their current paradigm, be it in the field of science or religion, is simply a description of reality and not reality itself. Few people are open to the idea that their current description of reality is not the only possible description. It is not an ultimate or absolute description but an approximation that was developed because people kept building on their previous understanding and beliefs. This lack of openness can spring from only one place, namely the ego.

If you look at the history of the Christian religion, you will see that during the development of the orthodox church, Christian beliefs, dogmas and doctrines were heavily influenced by the beliefs of the leaders of the church. One obvious example is the development of the Roman Catholic Church which was heavily influenced by the beliefs and political expediency of several Roman emperors. This is an undeniable fact that anyone can confirm by looking at historical evidence. Likewise, the development of modern science was heavily influenced by the conflict between the Catholic Church and early scientists. Had it not been for this conflict, scientific materialism would never have developed. If early scientists had not been so anxious to "get back at the Church," they would never have developed theories that "prove" there is nothing beyond the material universe.

On top of these considerations, you also need to consider the influence of the ego and how it causes people to become attached to certain viewpoints and beliefs. Your current knowledge will limit the kind of questions you are *able* to formulate, but your ego will limit the kind of questions you are *willing* to formulate. You see this most clearly in the field of religion where so many religious people refuse to consider any question that cannot be answered by their current religious doctrines. As a result, millions of religious people live their entire lives with numerous unanswered questions. This is not because these questions don't have answers; it is because people are not willing to look for those answers beyond a certain belief system, a certain mental box.

Even in the field of science you see many materialistic scientists who refuse to consider scientific data indicating that there might be something beyond the material universe. Neither science nor religion will reach their full potential until a critical mass of people become aware of this mechanism and decide to make a determined and conscious effort to overcome the manipulation of their egos.

The mechanism that drives humankind's growth is that people ask questions. The biggest hindrance to growth is that people allow their egos to make them attached to certain beliefs. Because of this attachment, people refuse to ask questions that go beyond their current beliefs. It should be obvious that when the driving force behind all progress is to ask questions, anything that prevents people from asking questions works against progress.

Going back to your original question of how this could change, the answer is that things will change when a critical mass of people decide that they can no longer live with certain unanswered questions. A great number of spiritual people have already decided that they cannot live with the incomplete answers they get from traditional religions, and they are looking for answers elsewhere. There is also a growing movement of scientists who are willing to look for answers beyond materialism. As these two movements gather momentum, and eventually merge, you will see dramatic changes in the fields of both science and religion.

I can see that science has a built-in safety mechanism because as long as there is data that cannot be explained by current theories, some scientists will

feel compelled to look beyond those theories. Is there a similar mechanism in the field of religion?

As I just mentioned, you do have a similar mechanism. People have a built-in desire to know, and they want to understand their relationship to God. They will not forever be satisfied by doctrines that provide no real answers. Go back to medieval Europe. You had a very closed society dominated by the Catholic Church. Any unbiased observer will admit that the medieval church had brainwashed the population and attempted to scare them into accepting official church doctrines without ever questioning those doctrines. Nevertheless, some people were not satisfied by church doctrines. These people could not stop asking questions. They realized that there were too many questions that church doctrines could not explain, and they refused to stop asking those questions. Some were willing to go to their death in order to defend their right, every person's right, to ask questions. It is exactly this mystical approach that is currently creating a great renewal in the religious life of this planet. Many people have abandoned traditional religion, yet they have not abandoned spirituality. You see many people who are becoming interested in the more mystical or spiritual aspects of their religion. When I appeared 2,000 years ago, you had a very similar situation. As I explained earlier, this is a product of the spiritual cycles and the release of a new type of spiritual energy. When new spiritual energies are released, some people immediately recognize the new energies and open their minds and hearts to a new understanding of the spiritual side of life. It is this spiritual or mystical drive that brings renewal to the religious life on earth.

Are you encouraging people to take a more spiritual or mystical approach to both religion and science?

Absolutely! The people who followed me 2,000 years ago were open to an understanding beyond orthodox doctrines. It is precisely this type of people that you today find in the New Age movement or in the spiritual and mystical movements of traditional religions. Who was it that persecuted me 2,000 years ago? It was precisely the type of people who today cling to orthodox beliefs, be they in Christianity, in other religions or in the field of science.

You will find many scientists who cling to orthodox scientific paradigms, such as materialism. Fortunately, there is a growing number of scientists who are taking a mystical approach to science. What is likely to happen in the coming decades is that the mystics in the field of religion and the mystics in the field of science begin to realize that they are not in opposition to each other.

When you take a mystical view, there is no contradiction, no conflict, between science and religion. They are, as I said earlier, simply two sides of the same coin. They are two different ways to describe reality, two different languages. As is the case with English and Greek, the two languages are not mutually exclusive. When you have a translation, people speaking the two languages can begin to understand each other instead of seeing each other as enemies.

Real change will not come from the religious and scientific establishments?

A major paradigm shift can happen only from the grassroots level, which is exactly the way Christianity spread through the ancient world. It can happen only when individuals begin to embrace and embody a higher state of consciousness. A higher understanding is the only way to bring about a paradigm shift. The shift will happen only when the top ten percent of the people recognize their potential to rise above the duality of the ego and put on their personal Christhood.

Both the religious and scientific establishments are currently dominated by the lowest ten percent of the population. They will, as history clearly proves, do everything in their power to prevent the widespread acceptance of new ideas. They will do this because they see new ideas as a threat to their power, which they believe rests on their ability to control the population. In reality, the population is controlled through consciousness. When the top ten percent decide to leave behind a certain limited state of consciousness, they will inevitably pull up the general population, and the "power elite" will lose some of their power. Although the lowest ten percent can delay the process, they cannot stop it. It is not a matter of "if" but a matter of "when."

I want to reach back to something you said earlier about people rising to a more rational state of consciousness. What type of consciousness do people need to attain in the next spiritual cycle?

They need to attain what one might call an intuitive, mystical or spiritual state of consciousness. The purpose of the rational state of consciousness promoted by science was to bring people out of the state of consciousness dominated by superstition and also to help them understand God's laws. In reality, the highest potential for the Age of Pisces was to raise people out of duality through the Christ mind. Because the orthodox Christian churches turned me into an idol, this did not happen through Christianity. Science was a step in the right direction because of its drive to avoid superstition. Unfortunately, science has also been influenced by the duality consciousness so humanity has not passed the spiritual tests of the Age of Pisces.

12 | Religion and Science

The invaluable contribution of science is the concept that it is possible to test your theories or beliefs through a systematic process. You formulate a theory and then you conduct practical experiments to test the validity of your theory. When done correctly, scientific experiments are not affected by the dualistic beliefs or opinions of the scientist. This is how science can help people rise out of the duality of the ego. I am not saying that a scientific observation and interpretation provides the final or ultimate understanding, but it *will* take humankind one step forward.

Today, most people believe that the process of repeated experimentation is a product of science. That belief springs from the conflict between science and religion. In reality, repeated experimentation is a universal principle that can and should be applied to all aspects of human endeavor, including the field of religion. The true mystics of the ages all engaged in a process of repeated experiments to determine the potential of the mind. It was this experimental study of consciousness that enabled many of them to rise above duality. Contrary to the idolatrous beliefs held by mainstream Christians, I was not born with the Christ consciousness. I had to work for it by walking the same spiritual path that everyone else is walking. It was only through repeated experimentation, whereby I stretched the limits of my mind, that I achieved Christ consciousness.

The problem with religion has been that virtually every religion has become a casualty in the age-old struggle for power and control. A small elite would take control of a particular religion, and the elite would begin to use that religion in an attempt to control the general population. As a tool for gaining this control, the elite created doctrines that defined what people were allowed to believe. These doctrines were not based on divine inspiration but on the duality of the ego, and therefore they contained many contradictions and unanswered questions. The leaders of a particular religion were not open to having their doctrines evaluated through a process of experimentation. They claimed that their doctrines were infallible and therefore above questioning. If you are not willing to put your beliefs to the test, you demonstrate that you are controlled by your ego. This is the hallmark of the lowest ten percent of the population—the power elite.

As a result of the growth into a more rational state of consciousness, more people are beginning to see through the claims made by the power elite (in every area of society). People are beginning to understand that religious doctrines are not infallible. Unfortunately, this has caused a lot of people to reject all religion, leaving them in a vacuum in which they have no sense of purpose or higher direction in their lives.

The true potential of the rational state of consciousness is that people can use it to reject "infallible" church doctrines without rejecting all spirituality and religion. Ideally, people should have used a rational state of mind to develop an understanding of the psychological mechanism that causes people to pervert religion in their quest for power. People could have used rational tools to remove man-made doctrines and establish an unbiased approach to religion, thereby rising above the duality of their egos.

The emergence of science did not make the power elite disappear from this planet, and there is still an elite seeking to control the population. Right now, their most powerful weapon for controlling people is scientific materialism. What is the real goal of this elite? It is to prevent any individual from attaining Christ consciousness and especially to prevent the emergence of a large number of people with Christ consciousness.

Look at how both mainstream Christianity and scientific materialism are promoting the same basic philosophy, namely that you as an individual are basically powerless and worthless.

Christianity said you are a sinner and that only Jesus Christ could attain Christ consciousness. Materialism says you are an evolved ape and that there is no such thing as Christ consciousness. Both are simply a denial of *your* Christ potential, and as I have described with the concept of a perception filter, people cannot co-create what they cannot imagine. The highest level of your perception filter is your sense of identity. If you identify yourself as a sinner or a sophisticated animal, how will you ever conceive of attaining a higher state of consciousness?

How can people apply the process of repeated experimentation to the field of religion?

I earlier said that science was meant to give people a rational understanding of the natural laws of God. This is extremely valuable, but it is only one side of the coin of life. The other side of the coin is that God also used a set of spiritual laws. We might say that the material laws are like the tip of an iceberg and the spiritual laws are like the ninety percent of the iceberg that is under water. How can you possibly hope to understand the material universe as long as you ignore the spiritual laws? Many material phenomena are simply effects of deeper causes that reside in the spiritual realm. This is the great limitation of materialistic science, and science will not go beyond a certain level until it acknowledges spiritual laws.

It will be difficult to study the spiritual laws through science as long as science is primarily using material instruments. One might say that as there is a horizon beyond which the human eye cannot see, there is a horizon beyond which material instruments cannot see. You cannot construct an instrument out of matter that will prove the existence of God because God is beyond all form. The spiritual realms are made of finer energies that cannot be detected by instruments made of the grosser energies that people call matter. People need to understand the spiritual laws as well as the natural laws. Material instruments cannot reveal spiritual laws, yet you can still use a scientific approach to study these laws. To use this approach, you need to find an instrument that can reach into the spiritual realm and reveal spiritual laws. That instrument is the mind, the Conscious You, which has the capacity to reach beyond the material universe.

As I said earlier, the mind is like a radio receiver. You can turn the dial of consciousness and tune in to different levels, vibrations or frequency spectrums in God's universe. The key to doing this is a mystical experience whereby you raise your consciousness above the duality of the ego. In the past, only a few people had reached a level of consciousness that enabled them to have such mystical experiences. In the new age, millions of people are meant to reach that state of consciousness. It will now be possible to study the spiritual realm through mystical or spiritual experiences.

Obviously, when one person has such an experience and uses it to start a new religion, which is later turned into an infallible doctrine, you run the risk that the original experience will be colored by the beliefs of both the prophet and succeeding church leaders. However, if a large number of people have mystical experiences, you can use scientific methods to compare such experiences. This opens an entirely new field for scientific inquiry. The possibilities are endless and could take science to a much higher level. Scientific study would not be performed exclusively through material instruments but also through the instrument of the mind. It has been said that space is the final frontier for science. In reality, the ultimate frontier is consciousness because everything is made from consciousness. One example of the fact that more people are gaining experiences of the spiritual realm is the large number of near-death experiences. I am aware that materialistic scientists reject these experiences. Nevertheless, for a person with an open mind it should be obvious that these experiences provide a useful glimpse into the spiritual world. So many people have had near-death experiences, and their experiences have been so similar, that an open-minded scientist simply cannot reject them all.

If people would use the rational tools of science and apply them to the field of religion, they would open new opportunities for increasing humankind's understanding of life. The true potential of the rational state of consciousness is to help people rise above the duality and the superstition of the ego. There are two ways to rise above this relativity. One is to study the material world through the unbiased investigation of science. Another way is to use the mind's ability to tune in to the spiritual realm. There is an outer tool for studying the material world and an inner tool for studying the spiritual world. Both are valid. Both have their limitations and their strong points. None of them can give people everything they need in order to attain a complete understanding of life. A higher understanding can be achieved only by combining both of the tools, both of the approaches to gaining knowledge. The coin of life has two sides. If you decide to ignore one side, you do so at your own peril. Your understanding of reality will inevitably be one-sided.

How could science and religion be unified?

By recognizing that neither science nor religion can be complete without a deeper understanding of consciousness. Religious people need to acknowledge that the true purpose of all religion is to help people attain a higher state of consciousness. Scientists must recognize that science can never be complete without incorporating consciousness. The current rejection of consciousness, based on the idea that consciousness is always subjective, is not sustainable. By reaching for Christ consciousness and combining it with scientific methods, it is possible to use the human mind to conduct a highly objective exploration of the spiritual world.

This change, this paradigm shift, must begin at the individual level whereby people start recognizing their ability to get viable answers from within. The key to changing the paradigms of science and religion is intuition, or rather Christ consciousness. Any true religion was started by a person who used his or her intuition to bring forth new spiritual teachings or visions. Intuition comes from the Christ mind and is part of what I called the "key of knowledge." Intuition and mystical visions must be restored in the field of religion. Many scientific discoveries came about as the result of intuitive insights, and some of the greatest scientists, including Albert Einstein, have acknowledged this fact. Intuition must be given recognition by the field of science.

Can you elaborate on the idea that science and religion are complementary ways to describe reality?

As I said, science and religion are two different languages, and currently only a few people have attempted a translation. The ascended masters serve as the spiritual teachers of humankind. For thousands of years, we have attempted to give people a progressively higher understanding of the reality of life. The greatest limitation we face is what one might call the language barrier. I do not mean words but concepts and images. Before we can communicate anything to human beings, they must have developed some understanding of the topic. They must have developed a language of concepts and images through which we can communicate a higher understanding. Imagine what it was like for us to try to communicate a spiritual truth or a higher understanding of the material world to a caveman. Then imagine what it was like to communicate with people in biblical times. When I appeared 2,000 years ago, people simply did not have a conceptual language that allowed me to give them the understanding I have given in this book. I had to teach in parables and I had to use concepts and images that people could understand. Consider how science has provided a sophisticated understanding of the incredibly complex functions of the human cell. How could I possibly have communicated the spiritual functions of the human cell to people in biblical times? Because people did not have an understanding of the material functions of the cell, I had no foundation for describing the spiritual functions of the cell.

Today, people have a more sophisticated conceptual language, and this gives the ascended masters an opportunity to communicate a higher spiritual understanding. What limits us today is that so many people have allowed themselves to become polarized into the two extremes of orthodox religion and scientific materialism. Neither camp is open to a higher understanding of life, neither camp is open to direct input from Above.

What needs to happen is that people begin to see the limitations of both approaches. When you realize that the teachings I gave 2,000 years ago were severely limited by people's state of consciousness and by their conceptual language, any spiritual person should be willing to let go of an attachment to the Bible. Any truly spiritual person should be willing to recognize the necessity of progressive revelation. Such people could then allow the ascended masters to bring forth more sophisticated spiritual teachings than what could be given 2,000 years ago. When scientists begin to recognize the value of their intuition and spirituality, they will realize that scientific discoveries can serve as a foundation, a rational foundation, for a higher spiritual understanding. For example, let us imagine that a scientist develops an extensive knowledge of the functions of the human cell. If such a scientist would make the effort to walk the path of personal Christhood, I can assure you that the ascended masters would begin to use that person as a messenger to bring forth an entirely new understanding of the spiritual aspects of the human cell. This would open the way for a complete understanding of the material functions of the cell, which are only partially understood today.

Once people begin to see that the rational knowledge developed by science can be used as a foundation for bringing forth a more sophisticated spiritual understanding of life, and that such an understanding can enhance the material side of life, science and religion will naturally begin to merge and fulfill their proper roles.

I still find it difficult to see how science could begin to recognize the mind as a valid scientific instrument.

I am far more optimistic. I don't see how science can continue to reject the value of consciousness, the existence of something beyond the material realm and the fact that the mind can serve as a bridge between the material realm and the spiritual realm. There are currently enough scientific discoveries, especially in the fields of biology, astronomy and quantum physics, that any open-minded scientist should be able to reach the only logical conclusion. Besides this fact, we have the – rather complex – topic of morality and ethics in science. Does the fact that something is scientifically possible mean that it *should* be done? Is there a point where scientists should refuse to do what is technically possible? Science cannot forever ignore the fact that scientists have become pawns in a game that aims at controlling the population, including the creation of weapons so destructive that it reduces both the scientists who create them and the people who deploy them to sub-human, immoral creatures.

Sooner or later, the scientific community will have to face the fact that without some kind of spirituality, science is morally bankrupt. Instead of saving the human race from the superstition of religion, science is well on its way to sending humanity into a downward slide of self-annihilation. The only possible way out of this dilemma is that scientists reach for the Christ consciousness that will allow them to be responsible scientists. This is the only way to prevent that scientists – many of whom belong to the top ten percent of the population – become blind pawns of the lowest ten percent, meaning people who will do anything to gain power.

The essence of the scientific method is that you must never stop asking questions. If your current scientific paradigm cannot answer your questions, you need to develop a higher paradigm. It is inevitable that scientists will eventually let go of scientific materialism. Even today, a growing number of scientists are beginning to realize and acknowledge the limitations of this paradigm. These scientists will gradually build a critical mass and a paradigm shift will occur. I sincerely hope it will happen within the next decade. I will prophesy that it will happen within the next decade, but because this is subject to the free will of human beings, my prophecy should not be considered infallible.

You make it sound like the separation of science and religion was a major problem for the growth in humankind's consciousness?

I do so for good reason. The war between orthodox Christianity and materialistic science has been the greatest setback for the spiritual and material evolution of humankind. No other single factor has had such a limiting effect on the expansion of people's understanding of themselves, the world in which they live and the world beyond. I can assure you that when people transcend the present state of war between science and religion, you will see such an expansion of consciousness that it will be beyond anything seen in recorded history.

13 | RELIGIOUS TOLERANCE

What do you think about the efforts to create better religious tolerance by fostering respect for other religions through dialog?

I am aware that many religious and nonreligious people are attempting to create religious tolerance and understanding through dialogue and by promoting respect for other people's religions. I do not want to in any way discourage such efforts. However, I must tell you that such efforts would have a far greater effect if they were based on a true understanding of the cause of religious conflict.

You cannot *impose* religious tolerance upon people; you cannot impose tolerance through outer measures. Tolerance cannot be forced; it must come from within. True nonviolence means that you have risen above the need and desire to use force. You cannot use force to free yourself from the desire to use force. You cannot pull yourself up by your bootstraps, you cannot use the duality of the ego to escape the duality of the ego. You can only transcend the duality of the ego and leave the ego behind. This can happen only through the Christ consciousness.

In reality, true tolerance must be based on a sense of oneness with all life. As mentioned earlier, you can have that sense of union only when you have a direct experience of oneness with your source. True tolerance is a by-product of the sense of oneness with all life. People must be helped to look beyond all outer divisions, such as religion, race, sex, ethnicity or nationality. They must be awakened to the realization that such divisions spring from the duality of the ego, and the only way to overcome conflict is to transcend the ego. However, people can come to this realization only through an inner experience of Christ consciousness.

Unless you attain the higher understanding and vision that can only come through the Christ consciousness, there cannot be true religious unity and tolerance on earth. If you are concerned about the need to overcome religious conflict, make an effort to raise your own level of consciousness. When you attain some measure of Christ consciousness, seek to inspire others to follow the same path. I am not here talking about making everyone follow a particular outer religion. I am talking about helping people who belong to your religion see that behind the outer doctrines and rituals there is an inner, universal path that leads to a higher state of consciousness. Only by following that path, within the context of their own religion, will people be able to gain a true respect for the members of other religions.

When you have followed the inner path, the mystical path, within your own religion and come to see the universality of that path, you will realize that people can use any religion as a foundation for the path. You realize that the true goal of religion is to help people attain a higher state of consciousness. It truly does not matter *how* they attain that state of consciousness. The only thing that matters is that they rise above the duality of the ego. You cannot create horizontal unity between religions. True unity must be vertical, meaning that it is built on the realization that all people and all religions came from the same source.

I assume you don't discourage people from different religions having a dialogue or taking other measures to promote religious tolerance?

No, such outer measures are very important, but such measures will not, in and of themselves, create the desired effect. For example, many Christians have engaged in a dialogue with those of other religions. After the terrorist attacks in 2001, many Christians attempted to reach out to Muslims. However, many such Christians still hold on to the belief that their religion is superior. They maintain a desire to convert Muslims to Christianity because they think it is the only way these Muslims can be saved. On the other side, the Muslims also maintain a belief that their religion is superior and the only true road to salvation.

A growing number of Muslims and Christians realize the need to avoid religious extremism that can lead to terrorist attacks or an outright war between Christian and Muslim nations. I am not saying there is anything wrong with these efforts. I am saying that as long as each side maintains its belief in the superiority of its religion, there are some real limitations to how far this can go. You will not truly *resolve* the conflict between Muslims and Christians. You might be able to attain an uneasy and fragile state of peaceful coexistence, but you will not attain true and lasting peace. The only way to attain such peace is to help a critical mass of Christians and Muslims rise above the duality of the ego. You can do this only by helping these people rise to a higher state of consciousness, whether you call it Christ consciousness or something else.

When you let go of the sense of separation that springs from the ego, you will feel as if an enormous weight has been lifted from you. You will gain an entirely new sense of self-worth. You will also be able to relate to other people in a better way. You will see them as equals instead of seeing them as threats to your fear-based need to feel superior. This need springs from a false sense of self-worth created by your ego. Instead of spending your entire life judging other people in an attempt to maintain your ego's fragile sense of self-worth, you can focus on being who you are. You can *be* and let *be*, meaning that instead of seeking to control others, you focus on helping them become more of who they really are. You don't accept yourself as a limited, mortal human being and you don't accept other people as limited and mortal. You work to help everyone rise above mortality and be who they are in God.

You say that it is the dualistic state of consciousness that causes people to go into the extremes and create conflict. Can you give a practical guideline for evaluating whether people have gone too far?

I can, but let me first say that one of the main characteristics of the ego is that it always wants to set up some kind of outer rule and turn it into a way to judge people. The ego thinks that as long as you follow the rules, you are always right and those who don't follow the rules are always wrong. This tendency is what leads to the extremes, the black-and-white viewpoints, that inevitably lead to conflict.

The only true guideline is whether your activities are based on love or fear. Fear will always pull people into one of two dualistic extremes, and this can only lead to conflict. Love will keep people on the golden middle way, the straight and narrow path (Matthew 7:13), which leads to the healing of all conflict through the mind of Christ. This is not the way of compromise between to relative extremes; it is the way of Christ discernment which transcends all duality. I have stated many times that the goal of the spiritual path is to take you beyond the duality of the ego. The best guideline I can give people is that when they feel they are being pulled into a polarized conflict, a black-and-white confrontation, they should immediately be on guard. Whenever you see a situation in which people have split into two factions, each claiming to represent the absolute truth and saying that the other group is completely wrong, you need to step back from that situation. I can tell you with absolute certainty that whenever there is a conflict between two human beings, none of them have the highest truth. I know this is a very direct statement. Nevertheless, the fact remains that whenever there is a conflict that divides people into opposing factions, the outer conflict has always obscured the truth that everything and everyone came from the same source.

As long as people are caught in the duality of the ego, they will always reason that one side of a conflict must be completely right and the other side must be completely wrong. This particular line of reasoning is responsible for more bloodshed than any other single factor. In reality, whenever two groups of people see each other as enemies, both sides have an incomplete understanding of the issue that divides them. This incomplete understanding springs from people's sense of separation from their source. If you are concerned about your own personal growth, you need to avoid being pulled into any of the dualistic, relative extremes. You need to step back from the situation and reach beyond the relativity of the conflict so that you can attain a higher understanding of the issue.

That is a pretty profound teaching, especially when you consider that religious people often get polarized

into such conflicts. I mean, throughout the history of the Christian church you see quite a number of such conflicts, and each side always claims that the other side is of the devil.

Yes, and as I have said before, it is precisely this attitude that leads to conflict and war. I can assure you that when people allow themselves to be pulled into such a dualistic conflict, both sides are helping the devil maintain his control over this world. If you claim to be working for God's cause, yet you see your fellow humans as enemies, you have taken a hypocritical viewpoint and you are supporting the devil. The devil's cause is separation and division. God's cause is harmony and oneness. There is nothing in between; you most choose whom you will serve—God or the devil. Will you serve the consciousness of separation and conflict or the consciousness of oneness and harmony.

Once again, the question is what you desire to see as the result of your personal involvement with religion. Do you want to come closer to God, or do you want to be pushed further away from God? In the spiritual realm we are all one. In the spiritual realm there are no conflicts. If you want to come closer to heaven, you need to rise above the duality of the ego because that duality is the only cause of conflict on earth. Let me say that again: "The duality of the ego is the *only* cause of conflict on earth."

That is why the duality of the ego is not allowed in the spiritual realm. That is why you cannot enter heaven without putting on the wedding garment (Matthew 22:12) of the Christ consciousness, which allows you to see through the duality of the ego. That is why I need millions of people who are willing to walk the path of personal Christhood and demonstrate their Christ discernment. It is only through people in this state of consciousness that we can end the current misery and bring God's kingdom to earth.

You have talked about a universal religion behind all outer religions. Is it correct to say that if a religion promotes oneness with God, it is an expression of that inner religion. If an outer religion promotes separation, it works against the true, inner religion?

That is correct. The true goal of spirituality is union with God. The Conscious You achieves this union by moving out of the dualistic consciousness and moving into the Christ consciousness. The goal of all true religion is to help the Conscious You make that journey in consciousness. Because it is an inner journey, there is more than one outer vehicle that can help you walk the spiritual path. The important point is that the outer vehicle helps you move toward oneness instead of keeping you stuck in separation. The key to making progress is to take the inner, or mystical, approach instead of the outer, or dogmatic, approach. No religion can guarantee your salvation, yet almost any religion can serve as a vehicle for climbing the universal path to God. The point is not the vehicle but how you use it.

There is an old saying that all roads lead to Rome. One might say that there are many roads to God. It does not matter which road you follow, as long as it leads you to the goal within your allotted time. The world's religions should be seen as roads to God, and in many cases they follow parallel tracks; they simply go through different landscapes. Some roads might be a bit bumpy and some might have obstacles. After you arrive at the goal, it really doesn't matter which road you took to get there. As I have said before, there are many beings in the spiritual realm who ascended from earth. These beings used many different religions to get here. We do not consider there to be one true religion or even a religion that is better than others. We recognize that people are different and that different people need different vehicles.

It would be simple to say that the best religion for you is the one that brings you home as quickly as possible. However, your personal path might have several stages. At various stages you might need different outer vehicles. The best religion for you right now is the one that can bring you to the next level of your personal path and can do so as quickly as possible. You might be able to follow the same religion for a lifetime, or you might need more than one. Even *that* doesn't matter as long as you move forward at maximum speed.

It is futile to fight over which religion is the only true one or whether one religion is better than others. To illustrate this point, let us imagine that we have a group of people who are lost in a dark mine. Their lamps have burned out, and they are fumbling around in the dark, looking for a way out. Suddenly, they come to a large room and see several tunnels that each have a light at the end. However, the tunnels have lights of different colors. Some of the people start arguing over which tunnel is the right one. Some claim that the tunnel with the blue light leads to heaven, while the one with the red light leads to hell. Others take the opposite position and they soon end up in a fight.

However, one person stands aside and starts thinking. She realizes that the color of the light probably isn't that important. The very fact that there is light proves that there is a way out of the mine. She starts walking down one tunnel and soon reaches the light at the end. She comes to a door made of colored glass. She opens the door and steps into the bright sunshine. She sees several other doors of different colors and realizes that the different tunnels revealed the same sunlight filtered through glass of different colors. She suddenly realizes that the confined perspective one has inside the mine no longer matters. Everything has become clear in the bright light of the sun. She opens the door and starts shouting to the other people in the mine. Unfortunately, they are so busy arguing that they pay no attention to her.

The question is simple: "Do you want to get out of the darkness, or do you want to stay there and argue about which way out is the only right one?"

You don't want to start a new religion but want to help people see the universal spiritual or mystical path behind all outer religions?

That is correct. There are more than enough religions on this planet. What is needed is universal spirituality. I desire to see every religion promote the universal spiritual path within the context and culture of that religion. Every religion needs to be brought into alignment with the true purpose of religion, namely to set people free from fear and dualism. To remain relevant in the new age, a religion must transcend the fear-based approach and sincerely help its followers attain the higher consciousness that allows them to reclaim their true identity.

The essential difference between religion and spirituality is that religion is focused on an outer organization, outer doctrines and outer rituals whereas spirituality is focused on an inner experience, a direct experience, of the spiritual side of life. As people gain more of these experiences, they begin to unify with their spiritual selves. Through that union, they will come closer to God, eventually attaining union with God. There is an extremely important message in the following statement:

> And he said unto them, The sabbath was made for man, and not man for the sabbath. (Mark 2:27)

As I have tried to explain, the original purpose for every true spiritual teaching is to set people free from the duality consciousness. Unfortunately, the duality consciousness can pervert and distort any spiritual teaching and turn it into a fear-based religion. When that happens, the outer religion is no longer a means to an end – namely to set people free – but it now becomes an end in itself. The purpose for the sabbath was to give people time to go within and make contact with their Christ selves. The "letter-of-the-law" people (what I earlier called the unbalanced organizers who have turned judges) made strict adherence to the outer ritual more important than its inner purpose. They actually lost the purpose for the sabbath because following the rules took people away from the direct, inner contact with their Christ selves as it does to this day. You see this theme repeated over and over in virtually every religion.

The process of turning a living spiritual teaching into a dead, ritual-based religion is always reinforced by the lowest ten percent of the people. This power elite will infiltrate a religion and use it to control the population through fear. Thereby, the goal of preserving the outer religion, and the power and privileges of its leaders, suddenly replaces the original goal of setting people free by helping them enter the kingdom of God within them. A religion has now become a tool for keeping people imprisoned in the kingdom of man, meaning the duality consciousness. The ruler of this worldly kingdom is the prince of this world whereas the ruler of the inner kingdom is the Prince of Peace.

The only way to restore a religion to its original purpose is to bring it back to its spiritual, or mystical, roots. Contrary to the claims made by orthodox Christianity, I was and am a mystic. The goal of all mysticism is union with God. That union transcends all of the outer divisions or categories found on earth. If you look at history, you will see that every religion produced mystics who attained some degree of union with God. Mysticism is a universal path that transcends all religions. However, most religions can serve as a foundation for the mystical path.

I am not suggesting that we create a new religion or that people abandon their current religion. I am suggesting that people from all walks of life take up the mystical path, the universal spiritual path, that leads to union with God. If you are a Christian, by all means follow the mystical path within the context of Christianity. In the past, many people have done so, starting with myself. There are a number of Christian mystics, as there are mystics in any other religion. There are also mystics who never followed any official religion, and this is perfectly viable. The only thing that really matters is union with God. That is why I said:

> But seek ye first the kingdom of God, and his righteousness; and all these things shall be added unto you. (Matthew 6:33)

The kingdom of God is the Christ consciousness and when enough people seek it, religious unity will follow.

14 | CREATING FALSE GODS

You have made a very clear case that the true goal of religion is to help us rise above the ego, which means that we leave behind all fear of God. When you look at the history of religion, I think it is pretty obvious that there has always been an element of fear in religion. Even today, so many people are affected by the fear-based approach. I would like to understand why there has been so much fear in religion? From as far back as I can remember, I sensed a spiritual being or Presence that was always with me. I never felt anything but love from that being, which always gave me the inner sense that there should be no fear in my relationship to God.

The presence you sensed was your personal Christ self, which many people see as their guardian angel. Most of the people in the top ten percent have had a similar experience, although many might have forgotten or suppressed it as they grew into adulthood. Other people have kept a connection to this presence in the form of intuition. For anyone who has such a direct connection, it should be easy to accept that you have no need to fear God, and there should – ideally – be no fear in religion. Unfortunately, almost ninety percent of the people do not feel this inner connection, meaning they are not consciously recognizing and using the key of knowledge. For these people it can be very difficult to see beyond the fear-based approach to religion, especially if it has been programmed into them from early childhood.

One can step back from the issue and say that there are two basic approaches to religion. The true approach is based entirely on love whereas the false approach is based on fear. Unfortunately, this view is only useful in an ideal world, and planet earth is currently a far cry from being such a world. Humankind's consciousness is currently at such a low level that it would be impossible to remove all fear from the field of religion. Fear will eventually be removed, but it will require that the top ten percent of the people raise their consciousness to a much higher level so they can pull up the rest of the population.

I have been an ascended being for 2,000 years, but some of my colleagues have been working as the spiritual teachers of humankind for much longer. When you gain a timeless perspective on the spiritual evolution of humankind, you become a practical realist. Think back to my example of a person with a college degree teaching math to kindergarten students. That person clearly sees the immense gap between college math and the students' ability to comprehend. Likewise, the spiritual teachers of humankind see the immense gap between the Christ consciousness and people's current level of consciousness. We do not spend much time on contemplating the ideal situation; we practice the art of the possible.

When we give a new spiritual teaching, we always design it for a specific level of consciousness. Over time, many cultures have become trapped in a fear-based state of consciousness, and fear always paralyzes people. When we release a spiritual teaching to such a culture, our first step must be to awaken people to the need to come up higher. No religion appears in a vacuum. In order to even consider a new spiritual teaching, people must be willing to look beyond their existing beliefs. Although these beliefs might be quite primitive, they often give people a sense of security and comfortability. Indifference to or fear of new ideas is often the toughest challenge for a spiritual teacher. It would be wonderful if all people could respond to us out of a true desire to grow and come closer to God. Unfortunately, people who are trapped in a fear-based state of mind cannot easily be motivated by love. We sometimes have to motivate them by playing on their fears. That is why you will see that there is much more fear in the Old Testament than in my teachings. Even *I* did or said certain things that played on people's fears. I did this partly to awaken people from their spiritual paralysis, but I also did it because until you make the fear visible, people don't have the option to overcome it.

When you consider this fact, you will see that we are often forced to take a calculated risk. If people are stuck in fear, a spiritual teaching that expresses only love will have little chance of appealing to these people. We must give them a teaching that uses their fears to compel them out of indifference and paralysis. Our hope is that people will become aware of the fears and use the spiritual teaching to rise above them. Unfortunately, there will always be some people who are so stuck in their fears that they refuse to confront them. Fear is always a fear of the unknown so until you look at it, you cannot overcome it.

People who are unwilling to look at their fears will focus on the fear-based aspects of a spiritual teaching. They will magnify anything that confirms their fears whereby they create infallible doctrines based on fear. When we start a new religion, we are very much playing the percentages. We know that a small percentage will be inspired to rise above their fears, another group will become even more stuck in fear and the majority will be raised a little bit without overcoming the fear completely. The problem is, of course, that after we give a spiritual teaching, it is usually only a matter of time before the lowest ten percent of the people begin to take over that movement and turn it into a tool for controlling the population. In this way, even a teaching with a high degree of love can – often within a few generations – be turned into a dogmatic religion, which presents God as a being to be feared. To be quite frank, the teachings I gave 2,000 years ago were ninety percent love-based and contained only enough fear-based ideas to appeal to people's state of consciousness. Over the past 2,000 years Christianity has been turned into a religion that is overwhelmingly fear-based and has relatively little love left. Yet, Christianity has still helped many people transcend fear and embrace love for God. Again, releasing a new spiritual teaching is a calculated risk, and because of free will, there are no guaranties. The duality of the ego can turn any love-based spiritual teaching into a fear-based religion.

> **That leads me to a question I wouldn't have dared to even ask a few years ago because I would have felt it to be blasphemy. I always wondered about the cultures with gods that demanded human or animal sacrifices and some of the instances in the Old Testament where God tells the Israelites to kill every member of another tribe or nation. When you consider that the first commandment is to "have no other Gods before me," it seems there is a real possibility of people worshiping false gods. Is it possible that there is a false god and that this false god might even have influenced the Old Testament?**

14 | Creating False Gods

I can understand that many people are reluctant to ask this question. It is not only a logical question to ask, it is an extremely important question to ask. However, let me make it clear that to answer it truthfully, I have to give you a very advanced teaching, which will be acceptable only to the most open-minded people. Let me first address your realization that in the past you would not have dared to even consider this question. If you want to grow beyond a certain point on the spiritual path, you need to rise above the fear-based mindset and develop such a love for truth that there are no taboos, no questions you dare not ask.

Why is that so important? It is important because the spiritual path is a process whereby you free yourself from *all* of the dualistic illusions that caused you to create a false sense of identity. You must be willing to lose your life, to lose your mortal sense of identity, by letting go of any and all of the dualistic lies that influence your consciousness and have become part of your sense of identity. In order to do that, you must be willing to question absolutely anything in this world, and then reach for an answer coming from your Christ self or from the ascended masters through your Christ self.

Consider the importance of the question of false gods. Let us imagine for a minute that there was a false god and that some people on earth had been fooled into worshiping that false god. If these people considered it blasphemy to even ask whether there might be a false god, how could they possibly be freed from that trap? They would literally be stuck for a lifetime and their culture could be stuck for thousands of years.

The basic law of this universe is free will. The ascended masters have been given the task of saving every human being on earth. To save people, we must liberate them from the dualistic illusions by giving them the truth that will make them free. However, in order to give people the truth, people must ask.

Ask and ye shall receive is a divine law (Luke 11:9). If you do not ask, you cannot receive from us because the Law of Free Will does not permit us to give you an answer for which you have not asked. Until you ask, you would not be open to the answer or able to bear that answer. You would use a dualistic viewpoint to reject the answer.

We must allow you to continue to live in illusion until you finally decide to throw away your taboos and ask the logical questions. In that respect, let me say that every religion which discourages its members from asking questions has been influenced by the dualistic lies and the forces that seek to keep people trapped in this world. There are no exceptions to this statement because it is the truth that will make you free, and the truth can be known only by asking questions. If your religion discourages you from asking questions, your religion has been influenced by the forces of this world. I am not thereby saying that your religion is completely false or is completely controlled by these forces. I am saying that your religion has been influenced by these forces and that is why it has created forbidden questions and infallible doctrines.

Think about this. Do you really think that human beings could ask questions for which God has no answers? Do you think the ascended masters are threatened by any questions people could ask? On the contrary, we have the truth that will set people free. We want people to ask the questions that allow us to give them a higher understanding of truth. Our desire is to set people free so why would we ever discourage people from asking questions? Only the power elite that seeks to control the population is afraid of people's questions, and only the prince of this world would discourage you from asking because he does not want you to be free.

Is there a false god? In reality there are many false gods. As I have attempted to explain earlier, human beings have created

14 | Creating False Gods

their own reality. The fruit of the knowledge of good and evil is the fruit of the knowledge of *relative* good and evil. Because human beings are meant to be co-creators with God, they have the power to create their own reality, meaning that they can create their own definitions of good and evil. Human beings can create a culture and a belief system on planet earth which is completely out of touch with the truth and the reality of God.

I am sure you can see that when people become trapped in such a relative belief system, they are worshiping a false god. The law of God mandates that when you create a relative definition of good and evil, when you create a "reality" that is out of alignment with the reality of God, you will be subject to the laws of deterioration that scientists describe as the second law of thermodynamics. This law states that in a closed system, entropy – meaning disorder – will increase until all ordered structures have broken down. The spiritual meaning is that a closed system is a system that is shut off from God.

God is love, and the nature of love is to flow, to self-transcend, to become more. In the material world, God's love must flow through people. If people are trapped in a fear-based approach to life, they will shut off the flow of God's love through them. Thereby, they will create a culture and civilization that becomes a closed system. Unless the top ten percent of the people transcend the fear-based mindset and become open doors for the flow of love, the civilization will inevitably self-destruct. That is why the current Western civilization is seeing an increasing number of problems that seemingly have no solutions. These problems will have no solutions until people rise above the consciousness of separation that created the problems.

As explained earlier, human beings partook of the fruit of relative good and evil, which truly means that they descended into a dualistic state of consciousness. That state of consciousness is dominated by the relative opposites of good and evil. These opposites are mutually exclusive, and they are different from the original polarities of God, namely the expanding and contracting forces.

As the Bible says, God created man in its image and likeness (Genesis 1:26). This means that God created lifestreams with imagination, with free will and with the ability to create by using God's energy. After human beings fell into a lower state of consciousness, they lost their conscious connection to the reality of God. It was inevitable that they began to create false gods. They began to create idols that were defined according to their own relative definitions of good and evil. They began to create gods in the image and likeness of man. They began to create gods that were an expression of their own state of consciousness. Those gods were "designed" the way people – or at least some people – wanted "god" to be. These people did not want to know the real God and its law. They wanted a "god" who lived up to their expectations and did not disturb their sense of being comfortable inside their mental boxes. People have now created a "god" in the image and likeness of their egos, and that god never challenges their egos.

How do people create a false god that can actually interact with them? As explained earlier, everything you do is done with God's energy. You are alive because there is a constant stream of spiritual energy which flows from the spiritual self through your Conscious You and soul vehicle. That energy becomes directed by your attention—by the Conscious You. As the energy flows through the four levels of your mind, it becomes qualified and colored according to the images, beliefs and feelings that you hold in your consciousness. One can compare this process to a film projector with the spiritual light being the white light from the light bulb that is colored as it passes through the film strip of your dualistic beliefs.

14 | Creating False Gods

As the laws of physics explain, energy cannot be created or destroyed. Once the energy is qualified by human thoughts and feelings, it will retain that vibration until those who qualified the energy raise its vibration back to its original purity. Where is the storehouse for the mental and emotional energy generated by humankind? I earlier said that the material universe is simply a spectrum of certain vibrations. The spiritual realm is made of higher vibrations, and there is another level of vibration between the material (visible) realm and the spiritual realm. This invisible realm is often called the psychic or astral realm. It is made of vibrations that are higher than the vibrations of matter, yet not pure enough to rise to the spiritual frequencies. This realm acts as a storehouse for the imperfect mental and emotional energy produced by humankind. If you take a look at history, it should not be difficult to see that there is an enormous amount of misqualified energy stored in this realm. Over time, many people have had visions of this realm. Some have seen it as a hellish place, and when drug addicts have a "bad trip" they actually contact this realm. Other aspects of the psychic realm are more benign and look almost like a heavenly world.

As the next step, you need to understand that as psychic energy begins to accumulate, it increases in intensity, and this leads to a logical conclusion. Everything is created from God's Being so God's energy is truly created out of God's consciousness. You use energy to create but you direct it with consciousness, meaning you embed a basic form of consciousness in what you create out of energy. As the energy begins to accumulate and increase in intensity, that consciousness is awakened. When a critical point is passed, a "cloud" of energy can attain a certain rudimentary form of consciousness. This mental and emotional energy now begins to realize that it exists. This has actually been discovered by science, namely as what Carl Jung called the collective unconscious. As psychic energy increases in intensity, the newly created entity or spirit can attain enough consciousness to realize that it can exist and grow only if it continues to receive energy from human beings. What has now happened is that, through the power of their minds, human beings have created a conscious being that exists in the psychic realm. Because this spirit was created by people's mental and emotional energy, it is connected to people's minds and emotions—people are tied to it in consciousness. This link is a two-way process, meaning that the spirit can influence – even manipulate – people's thoughts and emotions. Such a psychic entity can potentially communicate with people who are more than normally sensitive. Illustrations of this process are given in the book about Dr. Jekyll and Mr. Hyde and the book about Frankenstein's monster. People can create such a powerful psychic entity that it turns on them and starts controlling them.

Now add to this the fact that a lifestream can never fully forget its spiritual origin. The lifestream realizes that there is more to reality than the material universe it perceives with the senses. The lifestream realizes, even though it cannot put this into words or even conscious thoughts, that it has a higher self and that it will not be complete and whole until it attains union with that spiritual self. This is what, over the course of many millennia, has given rise to the concept of an external God, a God that is outside of, separated from and above human beings.

What truly happens is that when a particular group of people begin to form an image of such an external God, they will gradually create a conscious spirit that exists in the psychic realm. That spirit will naturally take on the characteristics envisioned by human beings. As it attains a certain degree of consciousness, it will begin to believe that it actually is the type of being that people envision as god. It will literally begin to

14 | Creating False Gods

believe that it is a god or that it is *the* god. The catch here is that this man-made god can continue to exist only as long as it receives energy from human beings. Because consciousness is by nature expansive, the man-made god not only wants to survive, it also wants to grow. As it attains a sufficient state of consciousness, it can actually begin to communicate with certain people and make demands concerning how it wants to be worshiped. It might prescribe certain forms of worship that cause people to give it more energy. If it was created as an aggressive god, it might prescribe animal or human sacrifices because by the spilling of blood, energy is misqualified and that energy is fed to the false god. In a similar vein, such a false god can entice people to wage war and to kill the enemies mercilessly, which is the real cause behind religious warfare. Once again, the spilling of blood through violence misqualifies energy, which can then feed the man-made god. Incidentally, this also explains many crimes performed by individuals, such as particularly brutal murders or serial killings. The minds of such criminals are completely taken over by a spirit in the psychic realm that feeds on the spilling of blood in violent crime.

I realize that many people will find this teaching very difficult to accept. If people are still trapped in fear, these ideas will seem so scary that they will refuse to consider them. People who have started to rise out of fear should be able to understand that no force in the psychic realm can influence people against their free will. Such forces can only manipulate you when you believe in dualistic illusions. The ultimate defense is to rise above such illusions by putting on the mind of Christ. One might consider that if indeed there is a false god, then you will never escape the clutches of that false god until you dare to question the validity of this "god."

If you find it difficult to accept this idea, there can be only one reason. Your religion has to some degree been influenced by a false god who does not want you to be free of its control. That is why your religious culture has instilled in you that there are certain questions you are not allowed to ask. This is especially true for cultures that contain the idea that certain questions about God are blasphemous and that you will be sent to hell for even asking the question.

The true God, whom I know and experience constantly, wants you to come home to its kingdom. You cannot come home as long as you are trapped in the worship of a false god. The true God wants you to overcome all illusions, and the only way is to question the dualistic lies that reinforce the false god. Those who do not want you to ask certain questions must have something to hide. Otherwise, why seek to discourage questions? The true God has nothing to hide. God is truth so why would God ever try to prevent you from discovering truth? If God wants you to find truth, why would it prevent you from asking questions that can lead you to the truth?

Only the truth can make you free. You live in a world in which almost every aspect of life has been influenced by dualistic lies. God has given you free will, and it has given you the right to question absolutely anything. You have the right to ask any question, and if you ask with an open mind and heart, the ascended masters or your Christ self will give you an answer that will help you free yourself from the dualistic lies. We are constantly offering you the key of knowledge, but you have to take that key, stick it in the lock and open the door to the mental box in which your mind is trapped. If you dare not ask, we cannot help you, and you will remain trapped until you decide to let go of your taboos and ask the logical questions.

For those who have a desire to know more, let me ask you to consider that the true God, the ultimate God, is a Being which is completely beyond the world of form. The Creator is more than anything it has created. God is complete,

14 | Creating False Gods

self-sustained and self-sufficient. God needs nothing from outside itself. How could the true God have a need to be worshiped by people or receive sacrifices from them?

This realization leads to a logical question: "How can a religion that promotes worship of an external God be a completely true religion? How can a religion that promotes worship of God be worshiping the true God who needs no worship?" God does not want you to worship it as an idol that is outside yourself. God wants you to enter its kingdom, which it has placed inside of you, inside your mind.

God does not want you to worship it; God wants you to become one with it. In reality, you are already one with God, for "without him was not any thing made that was made," including you. The true purpose of religion is to help you overcome the dualistic illusions that prevent you from accepting your spiritual heritage, your birthright as a son or daughter of God. Ponder and internalize these words:

> Beloved, now are we the sons of God, and it doth not yet appear what we shall be: but we know that, when he shall appear, we shall be like him; for we shall see him as he is. (1John 3:2)

If you dare to change your sense of identity and bring it into alignment with the reality of God, your Christ self will one day appear to you and show you the true Christ and the true God. You shall then see God as it is, and you will know that you are like God because you were created in its image and likeness. [For more detailed teachings on how we create spirits, see the book *Flowing With the River of Life*.]

In my experience many of the spiritually open-minded people are very reluctant to consider the existence of

a dark or evil force, especially one of their own making. Can you help me understand why?

There are two main reasons. The first one is raw fear. When a person is confronted with a danger from which it believes it has no defense, it cannot live with the resulting fear. Since the person thinks it has no defense against the threat, it can deal with the fear only by denying the existence of the threat. This mechanism has allowed people to live with the threat of nuclear war for over 50 years. Unfortunately, this has done nothing to remove the consciousness that causes the threat of nuclear war.

The only way out is to realize that all fear springs from ignorance. During the Middle Ages people feared many diseases and they thought they had no defense. As soon as people realized that some diseases are caused by bacterial infections, they discovered how to defend themselves and the fear dissipated. It is the truth that will make you free from fear.

In the case of evil, the key is to realize that since humankind fell into the duality consciousness, people have continued to co-create by using God's energy. What has been created from the consciousness of duality is an imperfect creation, and you can see some of that imperfection in the many forms of suffering found on earth. What needs to happen in this age is that the top ten percent of the people begin to understand that any form of human suffering is the visible result of a certain state of consciousness, and it is based on a dualistic illusion.

When you begin to gain the perspective of the Christ mind, you see that the key to removing suffering is that you separate yourself from the illusion that created it. You can then invoke high-frequency spiritual energy to transform the psychic energy back to a higher vibration. A true spiritual teaching is designed to help people escape dualistic illusions. Many spiritual rituals were designed to empower people to overcome suffering by invoking spiritual energy. If this was done on a sufficient scale, all imperfections could be removed, and then God's kingdom would be manifest on earth. As I have said before, the key to improving conditions on earth is that the top ten percent of the people begin to see themselves as an extension of the ascended masters—as Above, so below. This sets up a unique partnership, based on my saying:

> And Jesus came and spake unto them, saying, All power is given unto me in heaven and in earth. (Matthew 28:18)

The ascended masters literally have the *power* to remove all darkness and all suffering from the earth, yet we do not have the *authority* to do so. The Law of Free Will mandates that before a particular imperfection can be removed, a critical mass of people must separate themselves from the dualistic illusion that created the condition. I illustrated this in my parable about the tares among the wheat (Matthew 13:24). The inner meaning is that the tares is a symbol for the consciousness of duality and the wheat is a symbol for the Christ consciousness. When the top ten percent separate themselves from the consciousness that created a particular imperfection – such as religious conflict – then I can use my power and remove that consciousness from the earth. Until that happens, I can do nothing but watch as people continue to add to their own suffering. Although I have great compassion for people's suffering and would like to see it end as soon as possible, I am at peace in my total acceptance of God's law.

Let me now comment on the second reason many spiritual people ignore evil. These people have long ago seen through the fear-based ranting of hellfire and brimstone preachers, and they also see the hypocrisy of judging other people. They realize that many religious people are extremely judgmental, and they know this is not right because they have understood my saying:

> Judge not, and ye shall not be judged: condemn not, and ye shall not be condemned: forgive, and ye shall be forgiven. (Luke 6:37)

I would love to see these people realize that the judgment I spoke about was the dualistic judgment that springs from the ego. When you judge based on the ego, you will only add to the duality consciousness that keeps you trapped in a mental box. In order to escape that box, you have to abandon all dualistic judgment.

However, it is extremely important to realize that you should not fall into the trap of jumping into the opposite extreme. As I have explained several times, the duality consciousness sets up two opposite extremes, but none of them are right. In this case, one extreme is the judgmental attitude held by so many religious people, including many Christians. The opposite extreme is the attitude, held by many New Age and scientifically-minded people, namely that nothing is really "wrong." If the top ten percent adopt this attitude, they will literally be the good people who do nothing, and they will – by being passive – allow evil to triumph on this planet. The only way out of this dilemma is to realize that there is a higher form of judgment:

> 15 Ye judge after the flesh; I judge no man.
> 16 And yet if I judge, my judgment is true: for I am not alone, but I and the Father that sent me. (John, Ch 8)

When you rise above the duality of the ego, you can judge based on the Christ mind. This allows you to recognize the imperfections currently found on earth, yet you also see that they are simply temporary manifestations created from the duality consciousness. This empowers you to separate yourself fully from the consciousness of duality, which you cannot do until you recognize the existence of dualistic lies. Only then can you adopt the most constructive approach to evil, as described in my saying:

> Be ye therefore wise as serpents, and harmless as doves. (Matthew 10:16)

By adopting this attitude, you can recognize evil without becoming enveloped in it. You do not ignore evil, yet you do not seek to fight it from the duality consciousness. You allow God, or rather the ascended masters, to remove evil through you. For example, you can see that a person is trapped in a dualistic illusion without condemning the person. You will not label all followers of another religion as being of the devil. You will never label any person as being evil because you will understand that people do what they do as a result of being trapped in dualistic illusions. Instead of fighting against other people, you bring the truth of Christ to dispel all illusions.

Once a critical mass of people have separated themselves from a particular illusion, they can give the ascended masters the authority to remove that state of consciousness from the planet. This is what happened when slavery was abolished, and it is this very process that has brought all progress to this planet. There is literally no limit to how far this growth can go. The only limitation is people's ability to see through the dualistic illusions and their willingness to separate themselves from those illusions. Bringing God's kingdom to earth is not a utopian fantasy. It is a very real possibility, but it is up to the top ten percent of the population to bring it about by abandoning the beam in their own eyes—the egos that keep them tied to the duality consciousness.

Heaven can only wait. How long will *you* keep us waiting?

About the Author

Kim Michaels is an accomplished writer and author. He has conducted spiritual conferences and workshops in 14 countries, has counseled hundreds of spiritual students and has done numerous radio shows on spiritual topics. Kim has been on the spiritual path since 1976. He has studied a wide variety of spiritual teachings and practiced many techniques for raising consciousness. Since 2002 he has served as a messenger for Jesus and other ascended masters. He has brought forth extensive teachings about the mystical path, many of them available for free on his websites: *www.askrealjesus.com*, *www.ascendedmasteranswers.com*, *www.ascendedmasterlight.com* and *www.transcendencetoolbox.com*. For personal information, visit Kim at *www.KimMichaels.info*.

From the Heart of Jesus, vol 1

The teachings in this book have helped hundreds of thousands of people gain a deeper appreciation for Jesus's teachings about the mystical path that he taught 2,000 years ago and that he still teaches today—for those who are able to make an inner connection with him.

TODAY MANY PEOPLE CANNOT find a lasting heart connection to the real Jesus and his teachings because, according to most Christian churches, Jesus no longer talks to us. In reality, Jesus is a spiritual being and he is working to help all people who are able to raise their consciousness and attune to his Presence. For the past 2,000 years he has maintained a line of communication through those who have been willing to serve as messengers for his Living Word and who have pursued an understanding of his true message instead of settling for official Christian doctrines.

In this book, the ascended Jesus reveals the mystical teachings that he gave to his most advanced disciples. He explains why his true teachings are as relevant today as they were two millennia ago and how you can develop a personal relationship with him—one of the most remarkable spiritual teachers of all time.

Once you admit that mainstream religious traditions have not answered your questions about life, it is truly liberating to read the deep and meaningful answers in this book. Encouraging, moving and profound, this enlightening book will help you attain inner attunement with Jesus, even mystical union with him.

You will learn how to:
- recognize the silent, inner voice of Christ in your heart
- achieve permanent inner peace and happiness by getting connected with the Christ Consciousness
- heal yourself from emotional wounds
- get guidance from Jesus, who is your greatest teacher and friend
- communicate directly with Jesus

From the Heart of Jesus, vol 2

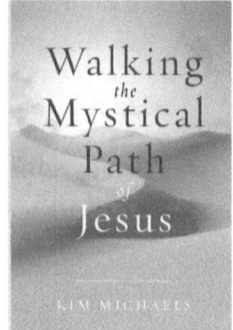

The teachings in this book have helped hundreds of thousands of people gain a deeper appreciation for the mystical path that Jesus taught to his disciples 2000 years ago, the path towards union with God, a state of mind beyond most people's highest dreams.

TODAY MANY PEOPLE HAVE trouble discovering the small, easy and practical steps towards a state of consciousness that is beyond human conflicts and pitfalls. In this book the ascended master Jesus describes how to start walking the mystical path that will eventually restore our most natural ability: the direct experience of God within ourselves.

This book empowers you to discover your personal path and make steady progress towards peace of mind and an inner, mystical experience of God.

Inspiring and profound, this enlightening book contains questions and answers that are easy to read and that help you walk the mystical path of Jesus.

You will learn how to:

- Use the cosmic mirror to speed up your growth
- Get out of old reactionary patterns
- Become free from difficult situations and guilt
- Control your mind
- Leave behind a painful past
- Open your heart to the flow of love from within
- Heal the wounds in your psychology

From the Heart of Jesus, vol 3

Hundreds of thousands of people have been inspired and uplifted by the profound teachings released in the form of conversations between the ascended master Jesus and Kim Michaels.

IN THIS BOOK JESUS DESCRIBES in a very personal way the more advanced stages of the mystical or spiritual path. Jesus describes through practical examples how our souls get fragmented in different embodiments and how the pieces of the soul get lost when we have experienced deep traumas in this lifetime or during previous lifetimes. The result is that our souls become vulnerable to different soul diseases that reduce our ability to enjoy life fully. Jesus explains how to restore our most natural ability—the ability to communicate with God directly. He skillfully explains how to make completely free choices in a world that seems to be full of toxic emotions and attitudes: fear, pride and guilt. Jesus explains how to overcome the sharpest tool of the dualistic mind—doubt combined with fear and pride.

In an easy to read question and answer form, Jesus guides you to a deeper understanding of how some lifestreams are young and mature, some rebel against God and some seek union with God. He helps you break through the opposition from both outside forces and the inner enemy of the ego.

You will learn how to:
- make use of your closest spiritual teacher – Jesus – on your own mystical path
- turn your past traumatic soul experiences into a forward step
- restore the fragments of your soul and by doing this developing your own direct union with God
- learn from even false teachers and overcome fear, pride and doubt
- avoid being disappointed by spiritual organizations
- create a new identity based on love

From the Heart of Jesus, vol 4

One of the most remarkable spiritual teachers known to humankind is Jesus who taught the mystical path of reunion with God to his disciples 2,000 years ago. Today, Jesus, as an ascended master, teaches that same path to those who are willing to be his modern disciples. Jesus knows that the major obstacle we all face on the mystical journey is the human ego.

THE EGO IS THE MOST SUBTLE CHALLENGE on the spiritual path because it distorts our thoughts, emotions, attitudes, even the way we look at life. In this book Jesus offers his most loving guidance in order to help you rise beyond the level of consciousness affected by the ego. In this newfound freedom, you will be able to grasp the divine vision, both for yourself and for the world you create.

Jesus teaches you how to start seeing through the illusions that the ego uses to keep you trapped in a lower state of consciousness. You will learn:

- How to avoid having your life consumed by an impossible quest
- How to distinguish between the ego itself and its illusions
- How the world view of the ego becomes a self-fulfilling prophecy
- How to rise above the black-and-white thinking of the ego
- How to avoid being trapped in the gray thinking of the ego
- How the ego can use a spiritual teaching to stop your growth
- How to overcome internal divisions that sabotage your growth

You will also find an in-depth discussion about why and how the ego was created. You will learn that you will always have an element of ego as long as you are in embodiment, but that you can come to see through the ego and make creative decisions.

From the Heart of Jesus, vol 5

A comprehensive guide to how you can avoid wasting your life on the fruitless games played by the human ego

TODAY MANY PEOPLE are trapped within tight boundaries defined by the ego games—the games of survival, security, power, control, competition, validation, responsibility and blame. With penetrating insight, the ascended master Jesus teaches that on our spiritual journey the human ego plays games that are very similar to the ones played by Frankenstein's monster: "The story of Doctor Frankenstein was inspired by the ascended masters in order to illustrate one of the fundamental properties of the ego. The plot is simple, namely that a doctor – with seemingly benign motives – stitches together dead body parts and infuses them with life. Once the creature has received a form of life, it displays a survival instinct that makes it willing to kill anyone standing in its way, even its own creator."

Jesus teaches through practical steps that spiritual rebirth requires us to voluntarily and consciously – if it is not conscious, it cannot be voluntary – let the old human identity die and accept that we are reborn into a higher spiritual sense of identity. You will learn how to:

- make LIFE decisions that turn your life experience positive
- recognize the ego games and the illusions that hold back your personal growth
- avoid having your life consumed by the ego's quest for security
- overcome the ego's survival, control, validation, blame and competition games and find true validation from your spiritual self
- take responsibility for yourself and stop feeling responsible for other people

"A person who controls the world is still inferior to one who controls his or her own mind. True personal power means that in any situation you encounter on earth, you can choose your reaction freely. Instead of reacting through one of the games of the ego, you can react by being the open door for your I AM Presence and the power of God." – JESUS

From the Heart of Jesus, vol 6

THE ASCENDED MASTER JESUS SHOWS you how fallen beings who oppose God have used the human ego to create the illusion of an epic struggle. The epic struggle, once it has engaged you, quickly becomes a personal struggle that traps many spiritual seekers in fighting for what they think is a good or spiritual cause.

In reality, the struggle is a complete illusion, or rather a drama, and it will never accomplish any spiritual purpose. It will keep you trapped in a downward spiral that feeds your spiritual light to forces that oppose God.

In this book, Jesus exposes with penetrating honesty how the false teachers have created a set of dramas that have enslaved people for a very long time. Jesus shows you how to pull yourself away from this false path and make progress on the true mystical path of union with your higher being. You will learn:

- how to recognize ego dramas and rise above them
- how to avoid seeking to prove one of the ego's illusions
- how to simply walk away from the drama consciousness
- how the ascended masters can help you escape your dramas and make true progress on your spiritual path
- how to escape the subtle illusion that God must have made a mistake or needs your help to fight other people
- how to reclaim your innocence

www.ingramcontent.com/pod-product-compliance
Lightning Source LLC
Chambersburg PA
CBHW030104170426
43198CB00009B/486